STRANGE TOPICS

Book #2

**Enigmatic Biblical Phenomena
with Possibility of Interpretation:
<u>Before The Flood</u>; <u>Genesis 5-7</u>.**

By José E. Espinoza © 2025

***BOOK #2 of The Series
"Strange & Controversial Topics
with <u>Possibility of Interpretation;</u>
In the Old Testament of The Bible"***

José E. Espinoza

Dedication

To a <u>Human Being Interested</u> in the Biblical Records of the Holy Scriptures, with the Desire and Purpose <u>to Know and Understand</u> the <u>Secrets of the Kingdom</u> of God.

- José E. Espinoza

José E. Espinoza

Content Page:

Table of Contents

José E. Espinoza

Introduction

Why do some tales from long ago still grip us, or draw us back for another look when everything else has faded? Perhaps it's precisely because they rattle the cages—speaking in riddles, hiding answers, blurring the lines between **what's known and what's possible**. The first chapters of Genesis are filled with these **strange topics**: people who vanish and are never seen again, names missing from genealogies, silent women standing at the crossroads of history, supernatural beings walking among us, rain falling for the first time to flood the entire planet, forests lost to memory, doors shut by God's own hand. If you've ever read these verses and thought, "What does this actually mean? Why is this even here?"—then you're in exactly the right place.

This book is for you or anyone who has felt frustrated by easy answers, who wants more than just the highlights. Maybe you're a young adult starting out in faith, and you want something that challenges your assumptions and **possibility of interpretation** about the scriptures. Maybe you lead a Bible study group or youth ministry, searching for passages that generate real discussion—not just nodding heads. Maybe you're simply someone drawn to puzzles, curious about

Enigmatic Biblical Phenomena With Possibility of Interpretation:

how old stories touch questions we're still asking: Who are we? How did society begin? Why does suffering exist alongside goodness? Whether you come out of conviction or curiosity, welcome—you belong in the circle of those wondering and yet willing to explore.

Genesis 5–7 (a world <u>before the Flood</u>) is often read with one eye on Sunday school flannel boards and the other on dramatic Hollywood retellings. But step closer, and you'll notice that beneath all the epic drama is a web of details so odd, so perplexing, so invitingly unfinished, that scholars and believers have been debating them for centuries. Adam lived for 930 years and had **"other sons and daughters"—yet we never hear their names. Enoch "walked with God—and was no more"**; his story suspends us between life and a kind of sacred vanishing. Did he die, or did something holier happen—something so outside the ordinary that it cracked open new ways of thinking about faithfulness, mortality, and hope?

The world before the flood was not just another chapter in an ancient chronicle—it was a place brimming with **mysteries** both spiritual and social. People multiplied and filled the earth. And as society grew, so did its complexity—and with it, controversy. Scripture introduces unsettling figures: of **Enigma/Controversy** with **the "sons of God"** and **the "daughters of men."** Their brief appearance in Genesis triggered debates as old as recorded theology. Were these daughters from Cain's line, marked by ambition and reputation? Did **the "sons of God"** belong to Seth's family—a remnant of faith—or were they something altogether different?

Then comes the flood itself—the pivot point where judgment, sorrow, mercy, and second chances meet. God announces a limit to human lifespans, setting the clock at **120 years**. Was this a reset button, a grace period, a warning, or something deeper about the nature of time and mortality? **Noah alone** stands firm, righteous in a collapsing world. Even the most tangible parts of the story invite speculation. Noah's Ark is built from **"gopher wood,"** a term that appears only once in the Bible. What was gopher wood? Was it cypress, cedar, **something now extinct?** Think about what it must have meant to trust instructions that didn't make sense, or even the gathering of **creatures who (for once) listened instead of scattered**.

Perhaps most poignant are the silences in Genesis—**the four women preserved through the flood, never named**, never given lines, but carrying the future inside them. What does it mean to stand at a turning point in history as an unnamed matriarch? And then there is the profound moment when **the door of the Ark is closed—not by Noah, but by God**. This is more than just shutting out the storm—it's a line drawn between old and new, between chaos and protection, between opportunity and consequence.

Finally, the flood waters covered the planet for **Elimination/Restoration (or renovation)**. The world is wiped clean—almost everything erased. A handful float in darkness and silence for 150 days, waiting for signs of life, hope, or simply dry ground.

If you are reading this introduction, you are likely someone who has sensed the **strangeness** in these stories and refused to look away. **Here, you'll find an invitation**: dare to read slowly, ask boldly, discuss openly, and carry the unresolved mysteries with you. **Every chapter ahead is designed to open space for conversation**, challenge, reflection, and sometimes even awe. You'll encounter perspectives from across history—literal and symbolic, spiritual and cultural—but always grounded in the text. Whether you're exploring on your own or leading a lively group, you'll discover material crafted to make ancient Biblical mysteries feel immediate and alive.

You won't find all the answers here. But you will find a road map through the wildest, most intriguing, controversial, and most neglected corners of early Genesis—places where faith meets uncertainty, where the unknown becomes an invitation, and where your own questions are not obstacles, but a vital part of the journey.

Step in, bring your wonder, your doubts, and your hunger for meaning. In exploring these strange topics together, we will discover that the very mysteries which make Genesis so puzzling are also what make it endlessly compelling, relevant, and even beautiful. **This is where possibility of interpretation** begins—not with certainty, but with courage, humility, and hearts ready to seek wisdom in **the strangest topics** within The Holy Scriptures.

Part 1:

Epoch of Piety

Attention!

A Remarking Note & <u>Clarification</u> from the Author:

To my readers, and with respect **to other biblical writers** and scholars, <u>let us remember</u> that when the Bible *says something, such as in Genesis 1:1, *"In the beginning God created the heavens and the earth."* It means exactly that as it is *written. Such statements do not require additional interpretation. Any other explanations are merely **possibilities of interpretation.**

-   José E. Espinoza

Chapter 1:

Strange

"Unnamed Descendants"

GENESIS 5:4

"After Seth was born, Adam lived 800 years and had <u>other sons and daughters</u>". – NIV (Bible)

No Names, just a Record of; *"Other Sons and Daughters"*

Imagine standing at the very dawn of human history, where a single family begins to grow into a vast community. The Book of Genesis gives us a glimpse of this early world through a brief but striking detail: **Adam and Eve had many sons and daughters** beyond the three we know by name. This quiet mention hints at a larger story of how humanity began to spread, develop, and create society from the roots of one original household. It raises questions that reach beyond names and numbers—questions about relationships, social order, and the roles each person played in shaping the earliest human experience.

As we explore this chapter, we will consider who these unnamed children might have been and what their existence means for understanding the foundations of human life according to Genesis. We will look closely at how families could have grown under unique conditions, how gender balance influenced survival and culture, and why these figures remain largely silent in the biblical record. By examining both literal and symbolic interpretations, we'll uncover fresh perspectives on Adam's legacy and the invisible contributions that built the first communities. This journey invites readers to deepen their appreciation of the ancient text and the mysteries woven into the story of humanity's beginnings.

POSSIBILITY OF INTERPRETATION 1:

Understanding this Strange Adam's Legacy and Societal Foundations

When readers reach **Genesis 5:4**, a curious statement stands out: *"And the days of Adam after he had begotten Seth were <u>eight hundred</u> years: <u>and he begat sons and daughters.</u>"*. Only three of Adam and Eve's children—<u>Cain, Abel, and Seth—are named</u>, but the text quietly places a '**multitude of unnamed sons and daughters**' **within the earliest story of humanity**. This passing remark opens the door to rich questions and creates a puzzle around the beginnings of the human population.

The simple statement about **<u>sons and daughters</u>** has logical consequences. One family stands at the head of an entire world. If Adam lived 930 years and fathered many sons and daughters, how many could there have been? If each child in turn lived for centuries, married a sibling or relative, and started their own families, population growth would accelerate rapidly. To picture this, imagine Adam and Eve as the root of a tree with new branches reaching out every year. If even just twenty-five children per generation married and had large families—possible in an age when lifespans stretched far beyond ours—thousands of people could arise in only a few centuries. That small beginning, like a single seed becoming a vast tree, matches what Genesis seems to suggest.

Turning to the genealogy, readers notice a curious **silence.** Genesis names only a few, <u>leaving out the stories of the majority</u>. Their absence hints at the priorities of the writers and editors behind the text. Named descendants—those forming the <u>thin line from Adam to Noah</u>—hold center stage because they carry the story forward, <u>shaping the narrative of faith and salvation</u>. 'The **unnamed, unrecorded offspring**' may represent the common folk of early society. Their toils fed the family, built shelters, and raised children, but they left no lasting mark in the genealogical record. Their roles echo through history as silent contributors; without them, society would falter, but their stories remain in the shadows. The recorder of Genesis, working within the customs of the time, focused on heads of lineages, not the everyday builders of human civilization.

Literal readings of **Genesis 5:4** see these unnamed sons and daughters as historical people, **the forebears of all future generations**. Their marriages to one another lay the groundwork for the first towns, crafts, and traditions. This approach asks: How did family groups avoid chaos? What morals or boundaries kept the peace? By contrast, a symbolic reading views the *"sons and daughters"* as representing **communal identity** rather than individuals. The phrase could stand for the richness of humanity, the potential within humanity for endless branching and growth.

Both perspectives guide readers toward larger questions: How did faith, memory, and purpose survive in such a large, shifting family? Each unnamed descendant, whether literal or symbolic, adds to **the foundation of civilization**—much like every branch of a tree strengthens the whole.

The growing population, teeming with children of both sexes, leads to fresh questions. How did the presence and roles of daughters affect the structure of early society? What patterns of marriage and work evolved as the population expanded, and what does this imply for the internal fabric of the first human community? **The possibilities stretch out, inviting deeper reflection** on balance, partnership, and the creative forces shaping those earliest days.

POSSIBILITY OF INTERPRETATION 2:

Exploring Gender Dynamics in Early Humanity:

More Men? More Women? Equal Number?

The story of Adam's early family surrounds us with the image of a population growing from a single couple into a thriving people. This process raises a natural question—how did the balance of sons and daughters within those generations steer the shape and survival of humanity's beginnings? Numbers alone would not guarantee thriving communities. A community's vitality rests on the mix between males and females, especially within a closely related family. Without a balanced ratio, growth would stall, relationships would become fraught, and the risk of harmful genetic pairing would climb.

Close reading of Genesis reveals that daughters, while seldom named, would have been just as numerous as sons. They provided the indispensable pool for new familial pairings and for blending genetic lines, both crucial for flourishing in the earliest days. Imagine a scene at one of Adam and Eve's family gatherings: daughters help weave new clothing, care for younger siblings, share in the cultivation of plants, and manage the fireside, drawing from a well of creativity and resilience. The ability to teach, nurture, and lead set the groundwork for new traditions. The unnamed daughters might have fashioned or passed down the first songs, healing remedies, or counting systems. In stories passed along, they could have become the caretakers of oral history, linking past and future.

Yet large numbers of sons could tilt the balance the other way. If there were more men than women, competition could emerge, shaping individual and collective behavior. Men might need to demonstrate skill or trustworthiness to form stable partnerships. In this setting, cooperative hunting or territorial defense could become highly valued traits. Storytelling might focus on bravery or leadership. Some sons, unable to marry within the close family, would look beyond their immediate group for partners, spurring early migrations, alliances, and cultural exchanges. Historical and anthropological research suggests that societies coping with uneven gender ratios often develop creative solutions to secure marriages and social harmony.

The fact that the Bible leaves Adam's daughters unnamed does not subtract from their hand in world-building. Instead, this omission invites imagination and curiosity. It calls the reader to ponder a hidden spiritual heritage, to honor the unseen, and to seek wisdom in stories half-told. Every unnamed daughter becomes a symbol for all those whose legacies survive in action and culture, if not in written word. Their invisible contributions breathed life into the first human society, echoing through time and tradition.

Summary & Reflection of this Topic

Now that we have explored the hidden depths of Adam's legacy through his **unnamed sons and daughters**, we can begin to see how these early family members shaped the foundation of human society in ways both <u>seen and unseen</u>. Their existence challenges us to think beyond the names recorded in scripture and to appreciate the vast and complex community that grew from one family. Understanding their roles helps us imagine the early customs, social structures, and balance needed for humanity to thrive. As we continue our journey through Genesis, **this mystery invites** us to reflect on the power of family, faith, and memory in building civilizations—and to welcome questions that deepen our connection to these ancient stories and their (possible) ongoing influence today.

Reference List of Chapter 1

Biblical references:

GENESIS 5:4

"After Seth was born, Adam lived 800 years and had <u>other sons and daughters</u>". – NIV

Other References:

First Human or First King? The Introduction of Adam in the Eden Narrative - Articles. (n.d.). BioLogos.

Genesis 5:4 - Verse-by-Verse Bible Commentary - StudyLight.org. (2025). StudyLight.org

Hagen, R. V., & Scelza, B. A. (2024, January 30). *SEX RATIOS AND GENDER NORMS: WHY BOTH ARE NEEDED TO UNDERSTAND SEXUAL CONFLICT IN HUMANS*. Evolutionary Human Sciences; Cambridge University Press.

Zhu, N., & Chang, L. (2019, July 23). *Evolved but Not Fixed: A Life History Account of Gender Roles and Gender Inequality*. Frontiers in Psychology

Chapter 2:

Strange

"Disappearance"/"Walk with God"

<u>**Genesis 5:24**</u>

"Enoch walked faithfully with God; then he was no more, because God took him away" – NIV (Bible)

Walking with God and Disappearing

Have you ever wondered what it truly means to **walk with God**? Can a life of faith lead to <u>something beyond the ordinary experience</u>, even changing the course of existence in ways we can barely imagine? What does it look like to stand firm in belief when the world around you seems full of confusion and doubt? These questions have intrigued readers for centuries, sparked by one brief but powerful story from ancient scripture. Exploring that story opens doors to deeper understanding about faith, devotion, and the mysteries that lie at the heart of spiritual journeys. This chapter invites you to consider not just the life of one figure from the distant past, but also the questions his experience raises for all who seek to know what it means to walk closely with the Divine Creator.

POSSIBILITY OF INTERPRETATION 1:

What Kind of Walk? Literal Physically? or figuratively?

Exploring Enoch's Walk with God

Enoch's life stands as one of the most intriguing narratives in the early chapters of Genesis. Unlike the other patriarchs listed in Genesis 5, the story of Enoch interrupts the familiar refrain, "and he died," with the distinct announcement that ***"Enoch walked faithfully with God; then he was no more, because God took him away"*** (Genesis 5:24). This short sentence has sparked much discussion and fascination across centuries, giving rise to two main interpretations about **what it means** to walk with God.

One way people have read Enoch's walk is as a picture of supreme spiritual faithfulness. Within this view, to walk with God means **to live each day in active obedience**, trusting and following the Creator even when surrounded by doubt and darkness. Instead of recounting the details of Enoch's deeds, the text points to the quality of his relationship with God. **Hebrews 11:5** picks up this thread, teaching that *"before he was taken, he was commended as one who pleased God."* His faithfulness becomes a model for persevering trust—a quality so valued that it draws favor from God. Many faith communities use Enoch's steady companionship with God as a pattern to aspire to, encouraging believers to remain steadfast, pursue righteousness, and maintain trust even in uncertain times. For those facing ridicule, loneliness, or the temptation to blend in with the crowd, Enoch's story becomes an encouragement to stand apart, drawing energy from quiet confidence and obedience. **Enoch's walk** shows that faith is not simply a moment of belief, but <u>an ongoing journey of daily choices</u> and continual trust.

There is another way to read Enoch's walk that adds a sense of wonder. This view hears the phrase as describing a concrete, almost physical companionship—suggesting that Enoch enjoyed a unique presence with God, not just in heart and spirit, but in experience. Stories from the early Jewish writings beyond Genesis, such as the Enochic traditions, take this **possibility** even further. These works describe Enoch crossing the boundary between human and divine worlds, entering heavenly realms, and being initiated into mysteries not even revealed to the angels. While the biblical text leaves Enoch's experience understated, later traditions suggest something much more vivid—visits to the divine throne room or a transformation into an angelic being. These stories (as **possibilities of interpretation**) invite readers to ask daring questions: Is it possible to walk so closely with God that the boundary between earth and heaven feels thin? Might spiritual faithfulness open up encounters and revelations beyond what we expect or imagine? While some readers hold back from literal interpretations, choosing instead to see these accounts as literary tools, others are drawn into the hope of real, extraordinary experiences with God in their own lives.

To understand why Enoch's walk drew so much attention, it helps to look at the world around him. The early chapters of Genesis draw a picture of a society drifting away from goodness, with violence and moral confusion spreading across the earth. Family lines grow longer, but **respect for God becomes rare**. Enoch lives in the generations between Adam and Noah, a time marked by spiritual dullness and **widespread injustice**. In a climate where death and compromise seem like the only options, Enoch chooses an alternative path—a life that stands out because of its difference. Instead of blending into his surroundings, he anchors his **choices and identity** in a unique relationship with God. While most formative encounters in the Hebrew Bible occur in the wilderness or on a mountain, Enoch's walk points to a life shaped by ongoing closeness to the divine, whether in public or in secret.

Enoch's devotion draws out questions about what it looks like to be faithful in the middle of confusion or decline. His narrative has become a touchstone for anyone trying to hold onto integrity when others drift away. Across centuries, faith communities have returned to Enoch's example, seeing it as both **challenge and promise**. The New Testament repeats his story as a model for walking by faith, and later mystical writings explore how his closeness with God might be possible in lives today. Enoch's legacy stretches beyond the moment of his departure, **encouraging readers <u>to keep seeking</u> <u>the Kingdom of God</u>**, even when the world feels disordered or hostile.

Questions linger about what exactly happened after Enoch's disappearance. **Did he experience a unique escape from death,** or does his absence symbolize something broader? These mysteries have only fueled curiosity in later texts and communities. Families living long after Enoch still remembered his life as a mark of hope—a reminder that faith and devotion can shape not only an individual's future, but the stories that echo through generations. This sense of expectation and curiosity sets the stage for exploring how **Enoch's fate** was received, and <u>what it meant</u> for those who came after him.

POSSIBILITY OF INTERPRETATION 2:

What Happened? Where did he go?

Understanding Enoch's Fate and Its Significance

In the generations before the great flood, Enoch stood out not only because he walked with God, but because of how his journey ended. Instead of dying like others in his family line, **Enoch disappeared**. The book of **Genesis 5:23** simply says, ***"…then he was no more, because God took him away."*** <u>This mysterious ending</u> sparks questions. Did Enoch die? Was he moved to another existence? Was this a form of ascension or a transformation into something new?

Looking closer at the biblical account, the letter to the Hebrews picks up this thread and gives it spiritual weight. **Hebrews 11:5** says that… ***"By faith Enoch was (*Translated or Transported) *taken from this life, that he did not experience death… "***. The Greek wording gives a sense that Enoch's translation or Transportation, was both a declaration to Enoch himself—that he had lived in a pleasing way— and a witness for others searching for examples of faith that matters.

The story links Enoch's fate to faith itself: ***"Without faith it is impossible to please [God]."*** **(Hebrews 11:6)**. For readers and groups studying these verses, Enoch's case becomes more than ancient history. It invites the question, what does it mean to please God, and what kind of reward or life can faith draw out?

Debate rises when thinking about **what God actually did with Enoch**. <u>Some hold that Enoch was taken physically</u>—his body and soul "translated or transported" <u>without seeing death</u>, **much like Elijah later on**. Others think of "translation" in spiritual terms, as a movement into another mode of existence or a foretaste of eternal life. This opens up space for reflection on the afterlife, and the mystery of what lies beyond ordinary human endings. Is Enoch's story meant to picture what can happen to a faithful person, or is it a unique marker unlike anything else in scripture? The story has echoes in New Testament ideas of resurrection and spiritual transformation that believers later hoped for. <u>Paul's letters, for example,</u> **in 1ˢᵗ Corintios 15:51-53** <u>talk about</u> **being "changed in a moment,"** or **"putting on immortality."** Enoch's experience offers an early, vivid symbol of these themes, showing that a walk with God can lead to new beginnings even when the path is hidden.

For Enoch's family, his sudden absence would have been life-changing. He had children and likely played a central role in teaching faith, sharing wisdom, and modeling devotion. His being taken may have left his family startled or searching. Did they interpret this event as a sign of God's approval? Did it lead his children to greater faith, or did the loss leave questions and new responsibilities behind?

Perhaps his vanishing would have challenged them to carry on the faith they inherited, and maybe even find new ways to seek God on their own.

Communities often have to adapt when a guiding voice disappears. In religious settings now, when a spiritual leader moves on or dies, families and groups face similar choices. Do they hold tightly to tradition, or does loss spark new growth and broader searching? The uncertainty surrounding Enoch's ending encourages young adults and study groups to talk openly about how to respond when faith roles shift or spiritual examples are gone.

Enoch's name also lives in other biblical and ancient texts (New Testament of the Bible). **Jude,** (in his one chapter brief letter) **verse 14,** for instance, quotes Enoch as a prophet who warned about the Lord's coming with *"ten thousands of his saints,"* showing that his legacy was bigger than is seen in Genesis. These ideas push readers to think about what it means to be human, to seek God, and to imagine life beyond what can be seen. Exploring these sources lets Bible study groups and individuals widen their understanding, find connections between old and new ideas, and ask thoughtful questions about the mystery of walking with God.

Summary & Reflection of this Topic

Enoch's life and **mysterious departure** invite us to consider how faith can shape not only a person's journey but also inspire those who follow. His example challenges us to remain steadfast in trust and devotion, even when the world around us feels confusing or dark. Now that we have explored the depth of **Enoch's walk with God** and the questions surrounding his fate, we can approach our own spiritual journeys with renewed curiosity and courage, seeking closeness with God in everyday life and remaining open to the mysteries faith may hold. Whether through steady obedience or bold wonder, Enoch's story encourages us to keep walking with God, knowing that such faith has the power to transform lives and generations beyond our own.

Reference List of Chapter 2

Biblical reference:

Genesis 5:24 "Enoch walked faithfully with God; then he was no more, because God took him away." – NIV

Other References:

Enoch in the Old Testament and Beyond | Religious Studies Center. (n.d.). Rsc.byu.edu.

The Heavenly Counterpart Traditions in the Enochic Pseudepigrapha. (2015). Marquette.edu.

Wolde, S. M. (2015, January 20). *THE HERMENEUTICAL CONSIDERATIONS IN THE NARRATIVE OF ENOCH: GENESIS 5:24*. Academia.edu.

Chapter 3:

Strange

"Daughters of Men" (who?)

Genesis 6:1-2

"Now when men began to multiply on the face of the earth and daughters were born to them, the sons of God saw that <u>the daughters of men</u> were <u>beautiful</u>, <u>and they took</u> as wives whomever they chose." – BSB

The Daughters of Men: Mention & Identity

Long before cities rose and kings ruled, a silent shift was underway in the early days of humanity. It began with simple glances—eyes drawn not by shared faith or common purpose, but by something far more fleeting: **beauty.** As these first unions crossed unseen boundaries, the foundations of society started to tremble. What seemed like innocent attractions soon carried the weight of <u>spiritual consequences</u>, challenging the very heart of devotion and obedience. This moment invites us to pause and ask: **<u>who were these women</u>** that stirred such change, and why did their presence signal a turning point in human history? Through exploring their identity, we step into a world where choices about marriage and lineage reveal deeper struggles between faithfulness and compromise—struggles that continue to echo through generations.

POSSIBILITY OF INTERPRETATION 1:

Connection to Cain's Lineage and Its Implications

Genesis 6 opens with a short, mysterious mention of the *"daughters of men,"* women whose marriages to the "sons of God" mark the beginning of a great spiritual turning point. Some scholars and teachers have identified these women as <u>descendants of Cain</u>. **The Cainite lineage theory** builds its case by connecting clues from Genesis 4 and observing how culture changed through Cain's family. Genesis 4 traces the lives of Cain's descendants through several generations, pointing out specific occupations and lifestyle shifts. For example, Jabal is described as the ancestor of all those who dwell in tents and keep livestock, Jubal as the father of all those who play the lyre and pipe, and Tubal-cain as the forger of all instruments of bronze and iron. These skills suggest growing expertise in both the arts and technology.

Cain's line became known for advancements that showed a mastery over their environment. Raising livestock meant developing resources beyond the subsistence farming of their parents. Metalworking opened doors to new tools and weapons. Creative arts like music flourished. These innovations pointed not just to development, but to a culture growing more concerned with human achievement and material progress. The focus on city building, with **Cain founding the first city** and naming it after his son, marks another step away from the simple, dependent life Adam and Eve had in Eden. There is a growing sense that the Cainites valued human pride, technical skill, and the ability to shape the world through their own power.

When considering the implications for the **Genesis 6** story, these cultural cues become important. The theory suggests that the "daughters of men" brought with them values stacked in favor of <u>ambition, power, and beauty rather than humble worship of God</u>. The contrast is often set against the **"line of Seth," who in Genesis 4:26** began to "call on the name of the Lord." Marriages between **the Sethites** (associated with worship and devotion) and the **Cainite women** created families whose values were no longer clear cut. The boundaries between faithfulness and self-reliance began to erode. Marriage, more than just a personal bond, became an <u>intersection</u> of worldviews—<u>one heavenly minded</u>, and <u>the other earthbound</u>.

Genesis 6:5 shows how quickly this blending led to spiritual decline: *"The Lord saw that the wickedness of man was great in the earth, and that every intention of the thoughts of his heart was only evil continually."* **Intermarriage** here becomes more than a romantic issue; it serves as a pathway for the spread of attitudes focused on power, comfort, and pleasure. To see how such mixing of values works in everyday life, imagine a faith community where the core group prizes simplicity, honesty, and service. Over time, as families marry into circles where status and possessions matter most, priorities shift. Simple joys get overshadowed by the need to keep up appearances. Little by little, spiritual focus grows fainter. The story of the **"daughters of men"** invites this kind of reflection.

The influence of **Cain's line** would not stop with individual values. Their expertise and visibility likely shifted social structures as well. When families produce **skilled craftsmen, musicians, and city leaders**, they amass wealth and favor. If these women were known for their social connections or outward beauty, they attracted interest from men in positions of authority. In antiquity, alliances through marriage fixed social boundaries as much as personal ones. Envision an early settlement where marrying into a line of metalworkers opens doors to resources or city privileges, while marrying a woman from a music-filled household means sharing in public celebrations and gatherings. The children born to these unions would straddle two worlds—one deeply devotional, one outwardly successful.

Competition and envy easily follow. Leadership might become the prize of those with the "best" connections. Power grows centralized. Cultural divisions deepen. In places where lineage equates to worth, resentment festers beneath the surface, and people wonder if favor and blessing are tied to family or faith.

Layered beneath the social story, however, is the theological question at the heart of the narrative: do these unions embody the age-old tug-of-war between holiness and compromise? **The mixture of Cainite and Sethite lines** brings to life the warnings found throughout

Scripture about <u>the dangers of **"unequal yoking."**</u> Relationships forged without attention to shared purpose drift apart or end in confusion. **When the godly join with the worldly**, the distinctive sound of faith weakens, setting the scene for judgment. The Genesis 6 story, seen through the lens of Cain's lineage, urges careful examination of how small steps toward compromise can have far-reaching effects.

As these questions rise, attention gradually turns to the personal traits that set these women apart. Their social vantage, family reputation, and the allure they carried raise questions about beauty and desire. What role did attractiveness play in these choices? How did notions of beauty and prestige shape the hearts and minds of those early generations? These threads invite readers to look even deeper into the mix of spiritual and cultural forces at work behind the scenes.

POSSIBILITY OF INTERPRETATION 2:

Beauty and Its Role in Human Relationships

The story of the '**Daughters of Men**' in **Genesis 6:1-2** opens a window into a world where lineage and legacy started to mean less than **fleeting attributes like beauty**. With earlier generations, spiritual legacy and family heritage held the highest regard, but the climate shaped by **Cain's descendants** slowly shifted these priorities. In that atmosphere, people began to measure worth and seek relationships with a different set of standards. What stood out most was the simple phrase, *"the sons of God saw that the daughters of men were beautiful."* This short statement says volumes about a society that had begun to judge value by appearance.

Ancient people saw physical beauty as a kind of power. Being fair or beautiful became something not only admired but also **desired**. In a culture moving away from godly values toward a celebration of style, the ability to attract attention or admiration through looks or appearance, grew more important than the strength of one's character. This was a turning point. As **the idea of beauty shaped choices** about marriage and family, people, especially men with influence, began to pursue relationships <u>based on what they could see</u> and the status it could bring, rather than on true partnership, virtue, or shared purpose.

When beauty became the yardstick for making decisions, families and marriages started to suffer. Instead of looking for qualities like kindness, wisdom, or faithfulness, men looked for outward features that fit the latest expectation of attractiveness. In this world, a woman's value depended on her ability to catch the wandering eyes of those who held power. Social status and favor came from appearing desirable, not from being wise or righteous. **As a result**, <u>marriages became less about lasting commitment</u> and more about **surface-level attraction**, causing families to weaken from the inside out and driving communities to place more <u>value in what fades with time</u>.

The shift toward idolizing beauty had deeper spiritual consequences. By making physical features a measure of worth, people turned away from the things that God values most. The Bible reminds readers that *"charm is deceptive, and beauty is fleeting; but a woman who fears the Lord is to be praised"* (**Proverbs 31:30**). When society makes beauty an idol, it distracts from the **heart-deep qualities that please God**—qualities like compassion, humility, and faithfulness. Practically, this kind of misplaced priority led to relationships based on self-interest and pleasure rather than love, trust, and spiritual growth. Over time, such attitudes eroded the foundation of godliness in society, opening the door for wickedness to take root and spread.

Looking at the world now, <u>the same patterns appear in fresh forms.</u> Today's culture is shaped by constant images of what is considered beautiful—**across movies, ads, social media, and celebrity news**. The cosmetics industry promotes flawless looks, while stories and images teach people, even from childhood, <u>to tie their value to how attractive they seem to others</u>. Recent research highlights that feeling inadequate in comparison to airbrushed images can push young people toward anxiety, depression, or even riskier choices like eating disorders and early cosmetic surgery. The power and influence of beauty, admired yet unattainable for most, leads some to measure themselves and others by shrinking standards that never satisfy.

Social media, in particular, breeds its own *"sons of God and daughters of men"* moment almost daily. An **endless scroll of likes**, hearts, and carefully posed pictures <u>creates a new kind of status</u>, often **defined by appearance rather than substance**. People may value themselves more for their reflection on a screen than for the kindness, help, or faithfulness they offer to others. This focus makes relationships shallower, raises pressure to conform, and can distract from the nurturing of character and spirit.

Faith communities have an opportunity to challenge this trend by praising what lasts. When churches and families encourage honesty, generosity, and humility—naming these qualities as beautiful—people can reclaim a sense of worth that isn't tied to appearance. In practice, this may look like parents affirming children for their courage or patience, or youth groups teaching that beauty, while real, is never everything.

By learning from the past, readers can ask, "What am I admiring? Who do I want to become?" Shifting admiration from what fades to what endures leads to meaning-filled relationships, a stronger foundation for communities, and a life that pleases God. This section of Genesis warns against making temporary things the basis for decisions that matter forever. Instead, it invites everyone to measure worth through the lens of God's heart, where true beauty is a matter of spirit more than skin.

Summary & Reflection of this Topic

Now that we have explored the possible identity and influence of **the "Daughters of Men"**, their connection to Cain's lineage, and the powerful role beauty played in shaping relationships and values, we are better equipped to understand how these early choices led to spiritual decline and social turmoil. Recognizing this mix of ambition, appearance, and faith challenges us to reflect on our own priorities and the ways culture still pressures us to value the temporary over the eternal. As we move forward, this insight invites us to seek deeper meaning in our relationships and communities—building on character and shared purpose rather than surface appeal—and to stand firm in faith amidst a world often distracted by fleeting charms.

Reference List of Chapter 3

Biblical Reference:

Genesis 6:1-2 *"Now when men began to multiply on the face of the earth and daughters were born to them, the sons of God saw that <u>the daughters of men</u> were <u>beautiful</u>, <u>and they took</u> as wives whomever they chose"*. - BSB

Other References:

Institute, M. H. (2015, June 12). *Physical Beauty and the Christian*. MD Harris Institute.

Chapter 4:

Enigmatic

"Sons of God" (Pre-Flood) Who?

Genesis 6:2

"<u>The sons of God</u> saw that the daughters of men were beautiful, and they took as wives whomever they chose." – (bible) – BSB

Topic of; "The Sons of God" <u>Before the Flood</u>

Who exactly were the **"Sons of God"** mentioned in **Genesis 6:2**? Why have these mysterious figures sparked so much debate among scholars and believers for centuries? What kind of influence did they have on the world just before a great and devastating flood changed everything? These questions have puzzled readers seeking to understand a passage that blends the line between divine and human in ways both confusing and intriguing. Exploring this mystery challenges us to think about identity, heritage, and the consequences of crossing boundaries—whether those lines are drawn by faith, family, or something beyond our usual experience. As we delve into the various interpretations, we will uncover how this ancient story continues to raise important questions about who belongs to God, what it means to live faithfully, and how choices ripple through communities and history.

José E. Espinoza

POSSIBILITY OF INTERPRETATION 1:

Exploring Lineage of Seth, and divine beings

Rival interpretations swirl around the mysterious **"Sons of God"** in **Genesis 6:2**, shaping faith and fueling debates over the centuries. **The Sethite interpretation** invites us to see these figures as the <u>descendants of Seth</u>, Adam's upright son, while their union with the **"daughters of men"** (understood as <u>from Cain's troubled line</u>) marks a **tragic intermingling of righteousness and rebellion**. This view carries heavy echoes of family dramas already woven through Genesis: Abel's murder, Cain's exile, the birth of Seth as a kind of new hope. The story drives home how legacy and faithfulness can either preserve or corrode a community's relationship with God.

Those who support '**the Sethite viewpoint**' to the moral divide traced across Genesis. The *"sons of God"* **inherit the spiritual promise through Seth**, the line meant to keep alive hope in darkening days. Their intermarriage with the *"daughters of men,"* instead of protecting their distinctive faith, **results in spreading corruption**, hinting at the collapse of boundaries meant to guard holiness. The story echoes earlier warnings about mixing light and darkness, and the outcome is not just personal harm, but communal drift toward chaos, ending in the greatest judgment: the flood. This interpretation explores how choices ripple outward, infecting whole societies. Even Noah, the sole righteous survivor, underscores that not all of Seth's line stayed faithful. The narrative raises real questions—how do people lose sight of their calling, and what does loyalty to a godly heritage demand? For the ancient reader, the boundaries of family and faith spell life or ruin.

The Sethite interpretation, though strong in connecting sin with human willfulness, meets resistance. Critics note that the Old Testament rarely calls human believers "sons of God," especially before the Exodus. The language carries more weight in talking about God's special covenant people, but Genesis 6 **uses "beney ha-'elohim,"** a phrase usually reserved for otherworldly figures. Some also argue that reading Seth's line as inherently righteous overlooks biblical realism—Cain's descendants were not alone in falling short. The flood narrative itself proves how deeply sin entrenched itself, affecting all families, not just one.

The competing view sees the **"Sons of God"** as divine beings, most often understood (or interpreted) as angels. Ancient Jewish readers and early Church fathers like Justin Martyr, Tertullian, and the writers of '*the Book of Enoch,' (*this book **not officially accepted** in the Biblical cannon), gave this interpretation vivid attention. In this telling, supernatural beings leave their assigned realm and trespass human boundaries, taking mortal wives and fathering the 'Nephilim'—giant, mighty figures set apart even in the age before the flood. Passages in books like Job and Psalms, some interpreters use "sons of God" to mean angelic or heavenly beings, strengthening the link, (as a possibility of interpretation). Even the translation of Genesis 6 in the *Septuagint, where "sons of God" (according to this *Translation) simply becomes "angels," supports this theological reading. The account in the book of **Jude: verse 14**, and the **2ⁿᵈ letter of Peter 2:4** also <u>looks back to angelic rebellion as a major reason for God's judgment</u> on the ancient world.

Looking to other ancient cultures helps unravel why this narrative carried so much weight. Mesopotamian and Canaanite myths feature stories of gods mingling with mortals, often producing heroes but also bringing chaos. Yet, the biblical writers place a different spin: the union brings not glory or new gods, but moral disaster and judgment. Whether focusing on <u>family lines</u> or <u>angelic trespassers</u>, both interpretations reflect deep anxieties about crossing spiritual boundaries—whether by breaking the chain of faithful living or by transgressing created order. For ancient audiences, holding the line between divine and human, sacred and secular, was as much about preserving identity as it was about avoiding disaster.

These interpretations press readers to wrestle with what it means to be human, how much harm can come from mixing or blurring boundaries, and what makes people responsible before God. The Sethite view nudges reflection on heritage: Are we masters of our destiny, or are we shaped by the inheritance we accept or reject? Personal faith, not just family history, becomes decisive. The divine beings view unlocks anxiety over forbidden knowledge or contact— echoing stories of those who dare too much and pay a heavy price.

Both challenge us about the cost of spiritual recklessness and the real dangers within and without.

Neither reading settles every question. The mysteries persist, inviting people to ponder, where lines should be drawn and what makes those lines worth defending. Real-world scenarios—an individual steering away from destructive influences, a community deciding how to guard its core values, or a seeker wondering <u>what it means to be counted among God's children</u>—echo the ancient dilemma. The text waits for new readers, inviting them to see themselves as those who could, perhaps, be called the **"Sons of God" by faith**, <u>picked out for a future shaped by hope and transformation</u>, just as the ancient stories once invited their hearers to wrestle with divine calling.

POSSIBILITY OF INTERPRETATION 2:

The Identity of Believers in Context

Ancient stories in Genesis show how being called a "son of God" marks someone as set apart, carrying weight in both honor and responsibility. This idea takes on a new form in the words of **John 1:12**, which says, *"But to all who did receive him, to those who believed in his name, he gave **the right to become children of God"***. These words connect identity not to lineage or status, but **with faith in Christ**. Here, being a child of God is open to anyone willing to trust and accept Jesus, not limited by birth or spiritual rank. This invitation to adoption signals a shift—the same way old stories gave significance to divine relationship; new stories invite anyone into that closeness through belief. With a new name and belonging comes the assurance that God's acceptance supersedes what the world thinks; it wipes away fear of rejection and gives a steady place in a sometimes-hostile world.

This new standing means the label **"son of God"** is neither distant nor academic but rooted in daily life and choices. Take for example the early Christians living under Roman rule. They were often outsiders, yet their faith gave them a sense of belonging that transcended public hostility. They called each other "brother" and "sister" because of this new family bond. Today's believers face other forms of pressure—mockery, doubt, even exclusion—but holding onto this identity can bring courage to live differently, to choose kindness, and to keep hope. Accepting oneself as God's child calls for honesty with self and others: if faith is more than a badge, it has to show up when values are tested, not just in safe spaces.

Living out this reality shows itself through both solo and group experience. On the individual level, someone might find comfort in prayer during tough times, or a quiet conviction that offers strength to speak truth gently. But the communal side cannot be ignored. When people gather as believers, the **"children of God"** idea takes on wider meaning—everyone belongs, with room to learn, care, and be honest about struggles. There are countless examples, such as churches organizing food pantries or coming together to support a family hit by a health crisis. In neighborhoods scattered by fear or loneliness, a group rooted in shared faith can offer connection, honest encouragement, and mutual accountability. Through this, everyone has a hand in building a culture where good choices are noticed, and support is always at hand.

With identity comes a higher calling. To be called a son or daughter of God is not just about privilege. It reshapes how choices are made—being honest at work even if others cut corners, standing up for a bullied classmate, or forgiving when it would be easier to stay angry. Tough choices do not disappear just because of faith. Instead, faith draws out the need to make character stand out even when it is hard.

Some days this means refusing to join office gossip. Other days, it means apologizing first when tempers flare at home. There are missteps and regrets, but also fresh starts and gratitude for the grace to try again.

The hope behind this identity is that people can change over time. Stories from the Bible and the present day show failures, but also second chances. Peter denied knowing Jesus three times but later became a leader of the early church. People today share stories of breaking habits, starting new patterns, finding peace after years of struggle. This ongoing process of being shaped, by love and faith, brings a sense that change is possible even when setbacks happen. Belief in Christ offers both a new identity (as sons/daughters of God), and the promise of spiritual renewal—old labels lose their power, and each step forward matters.

Anyone thinking about the meaning of **"sons of God"** can ask how this idea could shape their own choices, friendships, or sense of hope. The call is there: to belong, to show what God's love looks like in ordinary life, to lift others up, and to keep growing.

Summary & Reflection of this Topic

Now that we have explored the many interpretations of the **"Sons of God"** in <u>Genesis 6:2</u>, we are invited to move beyond ancient debates and consider what this means for us today. Whether seen as a call to honor our faith heritage or a warning about crossing spiritual boundaries, the story challenges us to think deeply about our identity and choices as people who strive to <u>live with purpose and integrity</u>. Understanding these complex images encourages young believers and communities alike to hold fast to their values, support one another through struggles, and embrace the hope found in <u>becoming true children of God</u>—not by birth alone, but <u>by 'faith in Jesus Christ' that transforms and renews</u>. This chapter opens the door for fresh conversations and personal reflection, inviting each reader to step into a living relationship with thc divine that shapes not only belief but everyday life.

Reference List of Chapter 4

Biblical Reference

Genesis 6:2 *"**<u>The sons of God</u>** saw that the daughters of men were beautiful, and they took as wives whomever they chose." - BSB*

Other References:

BEncouragement. (2023, June 8). *Understanding John 1:12: Becoming Children of God.* Lemon8.

Mrs. Crook (2025, March 23). *Exploring John 1:12: Understanding Our Identity as Children of God.* Lemon8.

Sons of God, Daughters of Men – A Mysterious and Controversial Bible Passage. (2025, April 18). Sound of Heaven.

The Sons of God: Three Interpretations of Genesis 6:1–4. (2024, May 3). Via Emmaus.

PART 2:

Times

of Tragic

Impiety

Chapter 5:

Strange

"120 Years"

Genesis 6:3

Then the Lord said, "My Spirit will not contend with humans forever, for they are mortal; their days will be a <u>hundred and twenty years</u>." – NIV (Bible)

Dilemma/Meaning of the '120 Years'

"Why did God say our days would be **120 years**?" This question has puzzled readers for centuries, stirring debate and curiosity among those exploring the ancient stories of Genesis. It is more than just a number—it touches on the heart of how time, mercy, and human life are understood in biblical teaching. The idea that God set a specific limit before judgment invites us to think about patience and choice, grace and consequence. What does it mean for people living in those times, and what can it teach us today about the way we use the time given to us?

In this chapter, we will explore what the 120-year period really means: a time full of opportunity but also a warning—a chance to turn toward something greater before the flood changed everything. We will look at how this time connects to human responsibility, divine patience, and the shift from long lifespans to a new reality where life feels shorter and more urgent. Together, we will uncover the deeper meaning behind this ancient promise and challenge, discovering how it shapes faith, hope, and our understanding of God's work through history.

POSSIBILITY OF INTERPRETATION 1:

Grace Period <u>Before Judgment</u>: Divine Invitation and Human Choices

God's words in Genesis 6:3, setting human days at **120 years,** often bring up the idea that this number represents a length of mercy before the flood came. The text presents the possibility of two paths: immediate judgment or a period to turn back, showing the kind of patience that lets people breathe and rethink instead of getting swept away at once. Instead of unleashing judgment right away, God gave the world time—a stretch long enough for generations to wake up or drift further from Him **(Genesis 6:3)** *"My Spirit Will Not Remain (or shall no strive) in Humankind Forever, since He Is Indeed Flesh (or mortal corruption); yet His Days Will Be One <u>Hundred Twenty Years.,</u>".*

This idea of a "grace period" taps into something deep about God's character. Instead of acting in haste, God lets the arc of history bend toward possible change. He waited, even when the world felt dark and relentless. The patience He displayed in those years echoes the hope that even when things seem settled or broken beyond repair, change could happen. The ancient world was not left without witness or opportunity. There was room for repentance, a window that made salvation possible for anyone willing to respond in those days, just as grace pulses throughout the rest of scripture (**2 Peter 3:9**).

During those years, the whole earth would have watched Noah build the ark, a project so impossible and large that it demanded attention. Noah becomes an image not just of obedience but also of personal witness—standing in the floodplain, building something for a world that didn't believe disaster was coming. The idea that Noah acted as a "preacher of righteousness and/or a vivid testimony," comes up in other parts of scripture, yet **the 'Genesis account gives no details about sermons or pleas'**. Still, the act of building and living so differently carries a message of its own. Imagine a man swinging a hammer day after day for decades, his life a billboard that reads: something is coming, make ready. Even if the words were few, every measured length of gopher wood was an announcement that things could change.

It's easy to picture neighbors and travelers pausing to ask questions or to mock. What is this for? Why build a boat so far from the sea? Noah keeps working, each day another chance for those around to watch—not just his hands, but maybe his heart as well. This echoes what it means today to stand out because of faith, to offer a warning or hope that most people choose to shrug off or ridicule. In every generation, there are voices, sometimes few, who call others to look up from routine and think of deeper things.

The 120 years stand out because they demand a response. Time itself becomes a gift and then a test. For the people before the flood, every sunrise was a chance to come alongside a message or to laugh it off. Here's where human responsibility steps strongly into the spotlight. The story points to free will—a deliberate space made for choice and consequence. God put the future of each person in their own hands; what happened next rested on countless ordinary decisions to listen or ignore, to think or press on with daily life. This sense of accountability runs right through the story: each person owned their answer, and the result echoed through history.

Beyond that, the passage shows that **God does not operate on our calendar**. His timing frustrates predictability. He chooses when to wait, when to act, and when to draw a line. If God took 120 years before the flood, it wasn't because He couldn't act sooner. He chose to create a stretch of days—a real deadline, full of possibility, but with the boundary clear. It invites readers to wrestle with why God sometimes lets consequences wait. What does it mean about Him? Is He distant, or more invested than we realize in giving people a real chance?

The idea of a ticking clock—a time of mercy that ends—remains challenging. It confronts people with the value of their own days. The end of 120 years didn't just signal judgment; it marked a new phase where lifespans would shrink and the world would never feel as open-ended again. When time feels limitless, warnings seem easy to ignore. But when the window begins to close, priorities shift. How does knowing there is a limit shape the way each generation lives their story and passes a legacy onward? As the ark neared completion, those choices moved from vague possibility to urgent reality, preparing the way for new boundaries on what it means to live, believe, and hope in God's world.

POSSIBILITY OF INTERPRETATION 2:

New Human Lifespan—A Threshold Change: <u>The Shift in Existence</u>

God's announcement of a <u>**120-year** limit on human life</u> emerged as more than a countdown to judgment. It became a dividing line in the story of humanity, marking the <u>end of an era filled with extraordinary ages</u> and the beginning of a world touched by the reality of death. Before this point, scripture names people like Methuselah living 969 years, Adam for 930, and Noah himself still reaching 950 even after the declaration (**Genesis 5:5, 5:27, 9:29**). The immense span of their lives shaped how people related to family, work, community, and God. Lifespans that stretched through centuries allowed individuals to witness multiple generations, carry memories backward, gather vast experience, and pass it all directly to children and grandchildren.

The sudden imposition of **a 120-year cap** brought a <u>radically different dynamic</u>. Genesis signals this turn when God observes that "My Spirit will not remain with mankind forever, because they are corrupt. Their days <u>**will be 120 years**</u>". The immediate context speaks not only to the approaching flood but launches **a new kind of existence** where time itself becomes precious and fragile. **The end of**

longevity removed the false security that there would always be "more time." Humans now faced their lives with a clock quietly ticking in the background.

This dramatic decrease in years did not come from simple impatience or arbitrary punishment. In the biblical understanding, a life with no foreseeable end exposed the dangers of ambition and pride unchecked by mortality. People had grown in power, knowledge, and resources to such an extent that their agendas often deviated from God's intent. With boundless time, ambitions could snowball, rivalries could intensify, and the temptation to live without limits became a threat. The story leading to the Tower of Babel captures how unchecked human drive can move entire societies to prideful projects—an echo of what happens when generations align solely around their own power.

A shorter lifetime draws boundaries around every ambition. No longer could plans take centuries to unfold. Dreamers had to choose what really mattered. Families would see their roots and branches enriched but also pruned. People who once knew their ancestors reaching far into the distant past now experienced history through the closer lens of parents, grandparents, and maybe great-grandparents at best.

Communities with accelerating generational turnover adjusted how they handled memory and teaching. The treasures of experience needed careful and rapid transmission, as time with elders became a fleeting resource. Many oral societies, both ancient and modern, carry this lesson at the core of their culture. When wisdom can vanish within a few lifetimes, customs of storytelling, apprenticeship, and shared rituals grow in importance. In early biblical history, tales of creation, the flood, God's promises, and the consequences of disobedience had to move from mouth to mouth with greater urgency. The people could not assume their ancestors would always be there to guide and correct them, so faith and knowledge demanded preservation through habit and intentional instruction.

Inside the home, children relied on hearing from their elders about God's faithfulness, promises, and warnings. The limits on life forced every generation to ask what must be passed down before time runs out. Just as travelers abruptly reminded of the setting sun hurry to finish their journey, families pressed on to instill faith, courage, and memory before another elder was lost.

For individuals, a briefer human lifespan fostered urgency and focus. **Life's meaning** now had to be discovered within decades, not centuries. The wise words of **Psalm 90** echo this theme: *"Teach us to number our days that we may gain a heart of wisdom."* The call to make every day count, to weigh decisions, to invest with purpose grew sharper when days became few rather than countless. People were drawn to treasure relationships, to mend disputes, and to seek purpose before time ran out.

Knowing that human life is bounded holds theological weight. It stands as a witness to the truth that we are not self-sufficient and that our ambitions must bow to a higher story. This was not a curse, but a constant invitation to humility and reliance on God's wisdom. Even giants of faith such as Abraham and Moses made their mark precisely because they walked their limited years with trust and obedience, not because they lived forever. Their stories show that, <u>in the face of mortality</u>, **greatness comes from living with meaning**, <u>not with endless days</u>.

Finite years offer the gift of intentionality. In every era, this boundary has inspired people to reflect on legacy, invest in community, and pursue spiritual depth rather than empty longevity. Whether in ancient times, medieval times, or today's world, **the limit announced in Genesis 6:3** <u>stands as a daily call to make our time count</u> before we hand the story to those who follow.

Summary & Reflection of this Topic

Now that we understand the significance of **the 120-year** grace period and the shift to <u>a shorter human lifespan</u>, we see how time itself becomes a powerful call to action and reflection. This era before the flood was not just about warning or judgment but about offering a window for change, a chance to choose differently amid growing darkness. The new limit on human life reminds us that our days are precious and finite, **<u>urging us to live with purpose</u>**, pass down wisdom quickly, and embrace faith with urgency. As we move forward in our own journeys, this knowledge invites us to consider how we respond to God's patience today—will we heed the call to live intentionally, share hope boldly, and steward the time we have as a sacred gift?

Reference List of Chapter 5

Biblical Reference:

Genesis 6:3 *"Then the Lord said, "My Spirit will not contend with humans forever, for they are mortal;* ***their days will be a hundred and twenty years****."* – (Bible) New International Version

Other References:

Genesis 6:3 Study Bible: The LORD said, "My Spirit will not remain in humankind forever, since he is indeed flesh; yet his days will be one hundred twenty years." (2025). Biblehub.com.

Genesis. (2024). Soniclight.com.

Matthew 1. (2024). Netbible.org.

Picray, S. (2010, October 25). *Did Noah Warn People About the Flood?* Words of Truth.

Chapter 6:

Strange "RACE":

(Humans? / Demigods?)

Genesis 6:4

*"There were **giants in the earth in those days**; and also after that, when the sons of God came in unto the daughters of men, and they bare children to them, the same became mighty men which were of old, men of renown". – (Bible) KJV*

Human Giants or Figures of Myth?

Long ago, beneath ancient skies, people whispered about <u>beings of immense size</u> and power—creatures whose presence blurred the lines between myth and memory. These were no ordinary men; they walked the earth with strength and renown that set them apart from all others. Their stories survived through generations, carved into scripture and legend, **inviting wonder and debate**. Were these towering figures truly giants, or did they serve another purpose in the tapestry of human history and belief? As we journey into this chapter, the echoes of those ancient tales challenge us to look beyond simple answers and consider what lies hidden <u>where faith meets mystery</u>.

Before The Flood; <u>*Genesis 5-7*</u>

José E. Espinoza

POSSIBILITY OF INTERPRETATION 1:

Exploration of Giants (Nephilim) as Physical and Metaphorical Figures

When the Genesis account says, *"There were giants (Nephilim) in the earth in those days… the same became mighty men which were of old, men of renown"* **(Genesis 6:4)**, it gives the first <u>taste of an ongoing enigma</u>: whether this race were truly giants who once walked the earth or figures of symbol and myth. The straightforward reading in both Jewish and Christian traditions leans toward the literal interpretation. It is said that 'this race' resulted from the union between the "sons of God" and the "daughters of men," introducing creatures possessing phenomenal height, strength, and prowess. This phrase, "sons of God," has spurred much debate, with some claiming it points to 'angelic beings', while others propose they are <u>descendants of Seth</u>, the righteous remnant of Adam's line. Their offspring, the Nephilim, seem to stand apart from ordinary humanity, marked by their might and fame—qualities that caught the notice of ancient writers who described them as monstrous, rapacious, and violent. Ancient stories in <u>Numbers and Deuteronomy</u> mention not only this giant's race (Nephilim) but the Rephaim, Anakim, and Emim, always as formidable enemies of Israel and, at times, legendary antagonists such as **Goliath** or **Og of Bashan**, whose iron bed became a symbol of unnatural size, according to **Deuteronomy 3:11**.

Skeptics—both ancient and modern—have questioned whether a race of true giants could physically or genetically exist. The tallest modern humans on record rarely approach eight feet, an outlier due to rare genetic disorders rather than a whole lineage. Current understandings of human genetics do not support a sustainable population of people double or triple normal human size. Giantism in known cases causes health problems rather than heroism. Critics point at this discrepancy and also question the secrecy that sometimes shrouds archaeological claims of giant bones or skeletons. Historians, like Herodotus, noted how misidentified fossils of great prehistoric animals often led to stories of giants, with the imagination of ancient civilizations filling gaps with formidable characters and/or mythology.

One alternative sees the story as tightly woven metaphor. Giants serve to reflect unchecked ambition, corruption, or spiritual decay; the Nephilim saga warns of the chaos that can unfold when boundaries break between the divine and the human, or, more simply, when power is left unrestrained. These "giants" become symbols of political power, moral challenge, or the dangers of pride. The tradition of using grand characters to teach lessons appears throughout biblical literature. Parables often rely on allegory: think of Pharaoh's hard heart, or the immense pride and fall of the Tower of Babel. In these stories, the "giant" does not need to be tall in stature but outsized in influence or ego, a figure whose downfall provides a lasting lesson to listeners of every age.

History is full of tales about mighty beings. Ancient Sumerians wrote about Gilgamesh, a legendary king with giant-like strength who sought immortality. Greeks sang of the Titan gods, immense and powerful adversaries overthrown only by wiser Olympian deities. In the Norse tradition, Jötnar were giants battling gods for control, while in the Americas, the Aztecs told stories of the Quinametzin, the giant builders of Teotihuacan who were toppled due to irreverence and hubris. Myths from across continents speak of larger-than-life figures—often credited with shaping the world or protecting great secrets, but always marked as "other," set apart from ordinary mortals.

Scientific perspectives emphasize skepticism in the face of extraordinary claims. No verified fossils or bodies have ever confirmed the existence of a "giant race." Some bones displayed as evidence turned out to belong to large animals, while occasional burials of exceptionally tall people reflect rare medical anomalies rather than a distinct population. Genetic research links height to multiple genes and environmental factors and establishes a clear limit on what human circuitry will allow. Any claim about a distinctly giant, hybrid race stretches far past these limits without fossil or genetic evidence to support it.

Despite these hurdles, the Nephilim story endures. Part of their draw lies in how they live at the edge of belief and skepticism—suggesting mortal ambition, the mingling of divine secrets with human struggle, and the tension between what is possible and what is imagined. Were they offspring of gods, cautionary symbols of corruption, or fabrications of awe-struck storytellers confronting a world too big to grasp? In stirring this ancient curiosity, the Nephilim invite us to imagine what it means to blur the line between mortal and divine, and to wonder whether legends of "demigods" might not be as far off as we once believed. The shadows they cast point toward larger possibilities still to be explored.

POSSIBILITY OF INTERPRETATION 2:

Examination of (Strange Giant Race) Nephilim as Demigods Across Cultures

The (Strange Giant Race) Nephilim have attracted deep curiosity because they appear at a crossroads where the divine meets the earthly, casting long shadows over questions of origin, faith, and destiny. **In Genesis 6:4**, readers encounter figures described as *"mighty men who were of old, men of renown"*—language that evokes something beyond ordinary human ability and invites comparison to demigods, the offspring of gods and mortals found in other traditions. **These biblical giants** are not merely tall or physically powerful; their mythic aura entices readers to ponder what it means when the boundary between the human and the divine becomes thin, or perhaps even porous.

Ancient cultures across the globe share a fascination with hybrid figures who blur the line between mortal and immortal. In Greek mythology, heroes like Hercules are born of divine and human parentage, granting them superhuman strength and destinies that oscillate between triumph and tragedy. The Epic of Gilgamesh, from Mesopotamian literature, introduces a king who is two-thirds god and one-third human—a ruler whose feats and failures echo the ambiguous legacy of the (Giant Race) Nephilim. These tales fulfill a longing to explain extraordinary ability or influence in human terms, using the language of divine ancestry. The Nephilim/Giants, depicted as warriors and great leaders, fulfill a parallel role in Hebrew tradition, demonstrating how stories of demigods reflect efforts to understand the extremes of the human experience—courage, power, pride, and hubris.

Old Testament references ground this archetype within Israel's cultural memory while glancing sideways at its neighbors' mythologies. Verses such as **Numbers 13:33** report encounters with this 'Giant Race' (Nephilim) after the flood, with Israelite spies describing the inhabitants of Canaan as giants—*"the sons of Anak, who come from the Nephilim"*—whose stature inspires awe and fear. This direct biblical testimony places this 'strange race' (Nephilim) in a line with the <u>mythical giants of other civilizations</u>, suggesting either a shared ancient belief in godlike ancestors or the use of allegory to convey spiritual truths.

Writers, theologians, and historians have often challenged the literal reading of this 'Strange Giant Race' (Nephilim) narrative. Many see the story as a metaphor, warning against the consequences of blurring sacred boundaries or pursuing forbidden knowledge. The imagery of divine beings mating with mortals echoes humanity's perennial temptation to reach for what lies beyond its grasp—the attempt to become like gods. In this perspective, the giant race (Nephilim) embodies the dangers of unchecked pride and the violation of limits set for safety and order. Some interpretations see their narrative as a caution that arrogance and rebellion against spiritual or moral law invite chaos, suffering, or even destruction.

These ideas find echoes in the names the Bible offers. "Nephilim" itself (as it is translated in most of the English version Bibles) can mean "fallen ones," possibly alluding to a descent from divine favor into a mortal, vulnerable state, or to a fall from grace resulting from transgression. (Even though, most of the Spanish Bibles translate them just as "Giants"). The Rephaim, often associated with the Nephilim, appear both as an actual race of ancient giants and as metaphorical "dead ones." The dual meaning underlines moral and spiritual lessons about mortality, remembrance, and the cost of greatness divorced from virtue.

Cross-cultural analysis deepens the conversation, showing how different societies have used tales of semidivine beings to examine their own struggles with faith, authority, and the unknown. Myths of titanic figures—whether Sumerian, Greek, or biblical—serve as repositories for questions about destiny, innovation, violence, and the human yearning for immortality. This comparative approach, underscored by sources like; McLoud (2022), helps readers understand that the Nephilim, while rooted in the Hebrew Bible, embody universal tensions that have shaped spirituality and myth across continents and centuries.

Within faith communities, the 'Strange Giant Race' (Nephilim) continue to spark heartfelt dialogue. In Bible study groups, their presence opens discussions about the nature of evil, the difficulty of interpreting ancient texts, and the reality or symbolism of spiritual warfare. Teachers and leaders confront questions from young seekers who see in the Giants/Nephilim both the excitement of legendary adventure and the sobering possibility of moral demise. Academics and laypeople alike debate how to reconcile these stories with contemporary values and historical knowledge. These exchanges do not diminish faith; instead, they encourage deeper humility and curiosity—qualities that energize spiritual growth rather than shut down inquiry.

As readers consider the Giants/Nephilim's lasting power, they encounter a story that is not easily contained. These ambiguous giants serve as reminders that the lines between literal history and myth, flesh and spirit, are sometimes difficult to draw. Their story pulses at the heart of religious and philosophical exploration, inviting both reverence and skepticism, wonder and sober reflection, into the ongoing conversation about what it means to be human in relation to the divine.

Summary & Reflection of this Topic

Now that we have explored the many faces of the Nephilim—as **giants**, as symbols, and as echoes of ancient stories shared across cultures—we can approach their mystery with both curiosity and care. Whether seen as literal beings or powerful metaphors, the **Nephilim** invite us to think deeply about the boundaries between humanity and the divine, about pride and humility, and about the ways ancient texts challenge us to explore faith beyond simple answers. This chapter encourages young readers, faith groups, and seekers alike to continue the conversation, asking what these stories reveal about our past and how they shape the questions we bring to scripture today. By holding space for wonder alongside reasoned inquiry, we open ourselves to richer understanding and fresh insights into timeless biblical mysteries.

Reference List of Chapter 6

Biblical Reference:

Genesis 6:4 *There were **giants in the earth in those days**; and also after that, when the sons of God came in unto the daughters of men, and they bare children to them, the same became mighty men which were of old, men of renown. – (Bible) King James Version*

Other References:

Aleksa Vučković. (2024, November 21). *Forgotten Giants: Were There Really Giants in Ancient Times?* Ancient Origins Reconstructing the Story of Humanity's Past; Ancient Origins.

McLoud, W. (2022). *The Nephilim, An Unholy Brood: Secrets and Enigmas of an Ancient Mediterranean Race (with bibliography)*. Creative Texts Publishers.

White, E. (2019, September 30). *Who Are the Nephilim?* Biblical Archaeology Society.

Chapter 7:

Mysterious

"Renown Men/Heroes"

Genesis 6:4

*"There were giants in the earth in those days; and also after that, when the sons of God came in unto the daughters of men, and they bare children to them, the same became **mighty men** which were **of old, men of renown**."* – (Bible) KJV

Powerful Men and of Renown

For centuries, the phrase "men of renown" has sparked questions and curiosity that refuse to settle into simple answers. **Who exactly were these figures** mentioned in ancient texts—warriors famed for their strength, leaders who shaped nations, or perhaps characters born purely from legend? <u>Their stories hover between history and myth,</u> leaving us to wonder where fact ends and imagination begins. As we delve into their world, we confront the challenge of understanding people who may have been remembered not just for what they did, but for what they came to represent across generations. This exploration invites us to reconsider how stories are told, whose voices endure, and what it means to be truly known in a time when memory and meaning often intertwine.

POSSIBILITY OF INTERPRETATION 1:

Warriors, <u>Leaders</u>, or Legends?

Ancient stories spark the imagination when they mention **"men of renown,"** a phrase that invites visions of mighty champions, **<u>great leaders</u>**, and living legends. Some thinkers suggest that these men might have truly existed as <u>powerful warriors</u>, remembered for their prowess on the battlefield. In ancient times, glory often belonged to those who led armies, defeated enemies, and <u>defended their people</u>. A single act of daring could become the foundation for legendary status, especially in cultures where storytelling preserved the memory of battles and heroes. The judges in Israel, like Samson or Gideon, started as individuals whose victories grew in the telling. Even outside the Bible, records from Mesopotamia or Egypt point to warriors whose deeds became the stuff of myth. Oral tradition, passed from parent to child, faithfully records the names of those who changed the balance of power, but it also leaves room for stories to grow with every retelling. Achievements become greater, foes become more numerous or dangerous, and weapons become enchanted in memory. This blend of truth and legend shapes our understanding of what it meant to be a hero, reminding us that ancient societies saw **renown**

STRANGE TOPICS. *Book #2*

as both earned and <u>amplified by the tales told about a person</u>. Some warriors may have begun as real people, memorable for their courage or skill, yet their reputations grew so large over generations that truth and invention merged into a single, magnetic idea of heroism.

The **"men of renown"** could also have been <u>leaders who shaped entire tribes or communities through their rule</u>. Early societies depended on strong organization and wise leadership just as much as on **military might**. Clan chiefs and kings often held absolute authority, controlling laws, resources, and even religious practices. <u>Their names had weight</u>, not just because of victories, but for the acts that guided their people's survival and prosperity. Evidence from archaeology, like inscriptions or ruins, sometimes reveals how a leader's reforms, alliances, or acts of justice changed history. These rulers might be remembered long after their reigns ended—not just for building cities or temples, but for founding dynasties or changing the way their people lived. The Bible gives hints of leaders whose words and deeds became legendary, and many ancient kings became half-myth after their death. Hammurabi's code, for example, shaped Babylonian society so completely that his authority echoed through the centuries. When storytellers spoke of **"renown,"** it could mean not just military fame, but also the far-reaching effects of decisions that shaped the course of nations. For many listeners, **stories of great leaders** were a way to pass on <u>lessons about justice, order, and wisdom</u>.

<u>Another possibility is</u> that (according some commentaries) the men of renown never lived as flesh-and-blood characters but belonged to **the**

Before The Flood; Genesis 5-7   **83**

world of pure legend. Across all cultures, people invent heroes and giants to fill the needs of the heart and mind. These legendary men serve as patterns of what a community values most: courage, cunning, generosity, or faithfulness. 'But it should not be ruled out that this topic is mentioned in the Bible'. Greek myths hold up Heracles as a picture of strength, while Japanese folklore remembers Momotaro as the protector of his people. Such tales are rarely about recording the facts. Instead, they serve as stories to inspire, to warn, or to unite listeners around a sense of shared identity. The men of renown in Genesis might be moral examples, crafted to showcase the rewards that await the faithful—or the troubles that follow arrogance or rebellion. Like Aesop's fables or ancient proverbs, their stories work best when they strike a chord in the heart and open the mind to reflection. They do not demand scrutiny as history, but they are powerful teachers that shape a society's memory and values.

Stories of men of renown could also function as powerful symbols, giving voice to hopes, fears, and common dreams. Societies often use certain characters to embody more than just personal qualities or individual heroics. The story of a fallen hero can remind people of the cost of pride, or a legendary lawgiver can become the symbol for justice that survived long after his laws faded. In the Hebrew tradition, the figure of Moses is more than a leader; he stands for the journey from slavery to freedom, for faith under pressure, and for the fragile bond between people and the divine. Legends persist not because they are proven, but because they let each new generation see itself reflected in the struggles and victories of the past. The men of renown can be seen as collective memories given human form, turnings points that every culture revisits when it wants to remember the ideal of unity or sacrifice.

<u>The mystery of the men of renown continues</u> to fascinate, not only because of who they might have been, but because of how their stories cross the border between fact, teaching, and symbol. The similarities and differences between them and mysterious groups like the Nephilim add to the puzzle. Readers may find themselves wondering where history ends and legend begins, where symbolism meets genealogy, and how the stories of the past keep shaping present conversations about identity, faith, and human greatness.

POSSIBILITY OF INTERPRETATION 2:

Link to the Giants (Nephilim) or Separate Group?

In ancient storytelling, characters often moved between history and legend, their real-life actions mixing with rumors and creative retellings. **Legendary figures** in the early chapters of Genesis exist right where myth and memory blur together. Stories about heroism, mysterious births, and almost superhuman strength became bigger than any individual, passed down through generations as both instruction and wonder. These men of renown, sometimes called **"heroes of old,"** invite readers to ask how much is ancient rumor and how much is narrative shaping a community's understanding of the past.

When looking at **Genesis 6:4**, the connection between the men of renown and the Nephilim stands out as a puzzle worth exploring. Genesis describes the Nephilim living on earth in ancient days, at the same time as the sons of God came into women and children were born: *"They were the mighty men that were of old, men of renown."* This wording brings up a question: are the men of renown and the Nephilim the same group, or does the phrase **"men of renown"** signal something new—a group that stands on its own?

<u>The possibility</u> that some renowned figures share a direct link with the Nephilim comes from clues in language and tradition. Both are associated with strength, the idea of "making a name," and an almost unnatural sense of greatness. In some Jewish traditions like 'the Book of Enoch', the Nephilim result from a crossing between celestial beings and mortal women, creating giants whose power and legend pass into later generations. Later, biblical enemies of Israel, like the Rephaim, are sometimes said to descend from these same beings, hinting that stories about strength, size, and notoriety followed families or tribes for centuries.

If the renowned heroes and the Nephilim are related, something interesting happens. Their stories might not simply celebrate physical might or fame; they could also carry warnings about the dark side of strength and the urge to dominate or "make a name." Divine power mixed with human pride often troubles biblical texts. Genesis suggests that pursuing fame outside God's plan leads to destruction, with the flood acting as an ending to the Nephilim's influence. The continued fear of descendants like the Rephaim fits with a legacy haunted by disastrous choices.

But a second reading sets these men of renown apart, making them new icons who do not repeat the mistakes of the Nephilim. Their narratives often contrast the **"fallen ones"** by following a path based on faith or humility rather than violence or rebellion. In Genesis, <u>after the flood silences the Nephilim</u>, the spotlight turns to figures like Abraham—marked not by might or divine parentage, but by a promise and a future given by God. In this way, men of renown could symbolize renewal. While "making a name" for oneself brought judgment to Babel, God gives a new name to Abraham, turning the focus from self-made glory to God-given purpose.

This deliberate contrast comes through in later Jewish and Christian interpretation, where legendary ancestors offer lessons in how to live well. Later traditions, including biblical commentary and folklore, wrestle with the legacies these figures left behind. Some see them as cautionary tales, while others consider them models for perseverance or faith. The confusion about their origin—were they born of angels or humans? Did they rebel or redeem?—creates room for debate, and sometimes for contradictory family trees or reputations. Readers and scholars still ask what lessons or warnings these blurry legacies offer to new generations.

Stories do more than just record facts; they get retold and shaped to fit questions about meaning or morality. In the ancient world, myth and legend filled gaps left by uncertainty. **Myths** tied to these men helped both warn and inspire. They merged stories of supernatural strength with examples of faith, adapting the original tales to show either a fall from grace or the hope of renewal. Heroes from the broader Near Eastern world—like Gilgamesh or Hercules—were often given similar makeovers, their foreign exploits being cautiously integrated or explained within Israelite tradition. When biblical writers pulled these ancient tales into their own story, they sometimes wrapped old legends up as examples of what not to do, or gave them an orthodox twist to fit within a monotheistic worldview.

<u>The puzzle of the men of renown</u> **does not have a single answer**. Their identity, whether shadowed by the Nephilim or standing apart, gives readers much to talk about. The ongoing discussion shows how myth, memory, and faith mingle in the stories that shape personal and shared beliefs. For anyone interested in the deep questions behind Genesis, the mystery itself is an invitation to think about what makes a hero and what kind of story a community chooses to tell.

Summary & Reflection of this Topic

Now that we have explored the complex identities and meanings behind the **men of renown**, we can better appreciate how their stories blend history, legend, and faith to shape our understanding of heroism and leadership in biblical times. Recognizing **the possible connections** with the 'Nephilim' (Giants) and the lessons these figures offer about power, pride, and renewal invites us to reflect on what it means to seek a true legacy. As we continue to study these ancient narratives, we open ourselves to deeper conversations about identity, faith, and the values that guide both past and present communities. This ongoing exploration encourages readers and groups alike to engage thoughtfully with scripture, welcoming questions and new insights about these strange topics, that keep these stories alive and relevant today.

Reference List of Chapter 7

Biblical Reference:

Genesis 6:4 *"There were giants in the earth in those days; and also after that, when the sons of God came in unto the daughters of men, and they bare children to them, the same became **mighty men** which were **of old, men of renown**."* – (Bible) King James Version

Other References:

Drummond, J. (2023, January 24). *The Nephilim and the Sons of God - Biblical Archaeology Society.* Biblical Archaeology Society -.

Jang, K.-E. (2025, July 26). *The Problems of Sons of Gods, Daughters of Humans, and the Nephilim in Genesis 6:1–4: A Reassessment.* Religions; Multidisciplinary Digital Publishing Institute.

Chapter 8:

Tragic "Lethal Choice"

(How/Why?)

Genesis 6:5

*"The Lord saw how **great the wickedness of the human race** had become on the earth, and that every inclination of the thoughts of the human heart was only **evil all the time"** – (Bible) NIV*

Iniquity as a Pandemic

What causes a society to slip into widespread wickedness? How do personal choices, community influences, and leadership shape the moral direction of a culture? In the world described in **Genesis 6:5,** the hearts of people were filled with evil continually—so much so that it marked a turning point in human history. Could this slide into darkness have been stopped or slowed? Are there moments when one person's decisions can change the course of many? These questions invite us to explore the complex forces behind moral decline, from individuals' actions to their relationships with others, and the impact of those in positions of power. Understanding these dynamics helps us think deeply about how communities hold—or lose—their sense of right and wrong. This chapter will guide you through these layers, revealing how personal integrity, social structures, leadership, and shared stories all work together to either protect or unravel a society's soul.

POSSIBILITY OF INTERPRETATION 1:

Could Evil Have Been Prevented?

A single person's choices ripple through an entire community, especially in moments when the stakes grow as high as **Genesis 6:5** presents. When the text declares that *"every inclination of the thoughts of the human heart was only evil all the time,"* it invites speculation about everything that could have slowed or stopped the world's slide into such a state. In the earliest pages of scripture, the possibility for one individual's uprightness to turn the tide stands out as a powerful theme. Think of Noah, who chooses righteousness in the context of widespread wickedness. His decision to obey spiritual principles sets him apart, and this choice influences not just his own destiny but the survival of humanity itself. Every day holds opportunities for small, ethical decisions—acts of kindness, honesty in speech, turning away from violence. If more people in the pre-flood world had made these choices, the momentum of corruption might have stalled. Cain's life shows the opposite side; his unchecked jealousy and violence become gateways for greater evil among his descendants. In this way, personal accountability becomes the front line. Embracing spiritual values—justice, mercy, humility—signals to neighbors a possibility beyond selfishness or cruelty. People watching each other catch glimpses of what they could become, for better or for worse.

Personal convictions alone fit into a wider structure built by the bonds of community. No person lives in isolation, and habits become customs as soon as enough people agree to them. In a world where neighbors check in on each other and families work together for shared good, the pressure to drift into wickedness meets friction. Imagine a village gathering at sundown for shared meals or rituals that repeat the values of honesty and peacemaking. When living closely, public accountability means actions rarely go unseen. Friendships turn into support systems, and the voice of community can call a wandering individual back before wrongdoing takes hold.

Mutual support and encouragement, brought to life in simple acts— helping a friend rebuild a house, joining together to protect the vulnerable, or even celebrating each small act that promotes unity— build up real defenses. In ancient Israel, for instance, the institution of the city of refuge weaves both justice and mercy into everyday law. The more communities make such practices ordinary, the harder it becomes for corruption to take root. Even the sharing of resources, group decision-making, and setting up elders to settle disputes can stem the spread of evil. Communities can serve as mirrors, reflecting back the shared values or magnifying the cracks. When these supports fall away, or when the group unites for the wrong reasons, trouble accelerates.

From the heart of the group rises the need for someone to model vision. Spiritual leaders—prophets, elders, wise judges—step into moments of crisis not just to warn, but to chart a better way. In times when Israel floundered, figures like Samuel or Deborah steered the people back to their original calling. These leaders draw from a well of personal character and expressive courage. Their influence spreads outward, shaping the expectations of what is possible and what is forbidden. A just leader can inspire an entire tribe to recommit to good, while a corrupt or silent one creates room for chaos and abuse. In Genesis 6:5, the lack of clear voices calling for repentance or reconciliation marked a dangerous silence. When spiritual guides flourish and step forward, their example can spark both reform and hope. If these voices fall away, the edges blur between what people will do and what they believe they should do.

Looking at what might have stood in the way of the widespread evil of **Genesis 6:5**, each layer—personal, communal, spiritual, cultural—offers some protection. When these break down, a different question emerges: Who failed to hold the line? <u>Which leaders faltered</u>, which narratives soured, and what lineages may have fueled the storm soon to break over humanity's head? These are the deeper mysteries that call for closer attention.

POSSIBILITY OF INTERPRETATION 2:

Impact of the Sons of God on Society

Influence often begins with the arrival of figures whose status, connections, or abilities stand out sharply from those around them. In Genesis 6, the narrative brings focus to **the Sons of God**, individuals whose presence shifted the social and spiritual tone of the surrounding community. Where moral boundaries had once come from shared memory or simple tradition, now society's character became vulnerable to the actions and priorities of those in power. When a group with unusual authority enters a culture, whether because of noble origins, spiritual significance, or simply visibility, the tone and outcome of the whole community change.

Scholars have debated the identity of these Sons of God. Some view them as the hybrid offspring of divine and human unions, casting them as supernatural beings whose arrival on the human scene represents a direct challenge to established order. (Williams, 2024). Others suggest that these figures stand for the descendants of Seth, regarded as a godly bloodline, who became entwined with the line of Cain, known for walking a less virtuous path. (Caputo, 2018). Still others view them as early rulers, tribal chiefs, or people of status.

Each theory brings different insight into how these individuals could have influenced every level of society. Whether their authority came from a literal heavenly origin or from inherited legacy, the lesson remains the same: when leaders lose touch with moral restraints, whole populations stumble after.

A culture often measures its values against the actions of its leaders and influencers. When those in power dedicate themselves to ambition, self-indulgence, or the blurring of boundaries once held sacred, the consequences reach deep into community life. In Genesis 6, the allure of the Sons of God expresses itself not only in their own rebellion but in the willingness of community members to copy or defend their behavior. Reverence for status often turns into permission for excess. Stories from throughout history echo this pattern, where rulers set aside restraint and, in time, their subjects justify or mimic the same indulgences. When the highest positions in society regard divine guidelines as optional, boundaries that once shaped behavior start to dissolve. What was once taboo can become ordinary or even admirable.

As this process continued in Genesis, the narrative highlights intermarriage between **the Sons of God** and **the Daughters of Men**. This crossing of boundaries stands as more than a personal choice; it marks the blending of two streams—one rooted in ideals or origins, the other representative of a broader humanity with all its contradictions and complexities. These unions had far-reaching effects. Where the sacred and the everyday mix, unchecked, clarity in belief and tradition often fades. The text speaks of the birth of the

Nephilim, described as "heroes of old, men of renown," **but their fame exists alongside accounts of violence**, <u>chaos, and loss of spiritual direction.</u> The community faces a dilemma: hold onto past distinctions or adjust to a new norm shaped by the ambitions and desires of its most visible members.

Cultural memory holds other examples of similar change. When Solomon married women from other nations, the entrance of new customs and beliefs pulled the people of Israel away from their own covenants, introducing confusion and divided loyalties. Egypt's period of Hyksos rule brought foreign gods and customs into everyday life, leaving a legacy of blended traditions and a loss of clear identity. When the lines between sacred obligation and personal will become blurred by those with the greatest influence, society drifts from its foundations.

The story in Genesis 6 also invites reflection on the deeper meaning of spiritual rebellion. Every act of insubordination by the Sons of God signals a deep refusal to trust or submit to the structures of divine order, sending a powerful message to all who witness their choices. **Rebellion** in this context is more than rule-breaking. It becomes an assertion that personal or group desire carries greater weight than the spiritual principles meant to guide everyone. When a society watches powerful figures elevate their own will above the covenant, respect for sacred boundaries breaks down everywhere. The fallout is not just personal but generational, with the aftermath rippling through families, traditions, and whole eras.

Standards erode. Trust between people and the divine weakens. Once these rebellious acts become normalized, the door opens for cycles of lawlessness, confusion, and even violence, as described in Genesis' account of **rising wickedness**. Spiritual structures built to promote justice and flourishing fall apart, replaced by a restlessness that forgets old hopes and codes. As the ancient text and later interpreters point out, such breakdowns are neither sudden nor accidental. They trace back to visible examples, cultural shifts, and the personal ambitions of those placed to influence everyone else.

Summary & Reflection of this Topic

Now that we have explored the complex layers leading to the **moral decline** described in **Genesis 6:5**—from individual choices and community bonds to leadership failures and cultural shifts—we can better understand <u>how fragile the balance between good and evil truly is</u>. Recognizing the power of personal responsibility, the strength found in supportive communities, and the influence of leaders and stories, challenges us to remain vigilant in our own lives and societies. By learning from these ancient lessons, young readers and faith groups alike can engage more deeply with biblical mysteries and encourage conversations that inspire hope, accountability, and a renewed commitment to values that protect and uplift. This awareness equips us to face today's challenges with wisdom drawn from those early, pivotal moments and to seek paths that resist decline and promote lasting flourishing.

Reference List of Chapter 8

Genesis 6:5 *"The Lord saw how **great the wickedness of the human race** had become on the earth, and that every inclination of the thoughts of the human heart was only **evil all the time"** – (Bible) New International Version*

Other References:

Caputo, N. (2018, February). *Sons of God, Daughters of Man, and the Formation of Human Society in Nahmanides's Exegesis*. Academia.edu.

Williams, G. (2024, December 4). *Sons of God and the Nephilim*. Academia.edu.

Chapter 9:

Enigmatic

"Repentance of God"

Genesis 6:6-7

*"**And it 'repented' The LORD** that he had made man on the earth, and it grieved at his heart." 7 And **The LORD said**,... ... for '**It repenteth me**' that I have made them.".* – (Bible) KJV

José E. Espinoza

A Repentance of The All-knowing God

Have you ever wondered how a perfect and all-knowing **God might experience regret/repent?** What does it mean when scripture says that God's heart was filled with pain over the way humanity turned out? Can a divine being, who sees everything and knows every outcome, truly feel sorrow or change direction? These questions challenge simple ideas about God and invite us to explore something deeply mysterious about the relationship between the Creator and creation. In this chapter, we will consider what it means for God to grieve, not as a sign of weakness or mistake, but as **an expression of profound love and engagement** with the world. By asking these questions, readers are invited to rethink the nature of God's emotions and what they reveal about His connection to humanity.

POSSIBILITY OF INTERPRETATION 1:

Exploring the Nature of Divine Regret/Repent

Genesis 6:6 disrupts simple views of God by saying, *"**The Lord repented/regretted** that he had made man on the earth, and <u>his heart was filled with pain</u>."* The passage challenges anyone who assumes God is unemotional or untouched by human life. Readers approaching this verse often carry the expectation that regret, when attached to a being who knows everything, hints at a mistake or change of mind. <u>Human regret usually means we wish we had done something differently</u>, often because of incomplete information or a sudden realization. But **divine repent/regret presents something far more mysterious**. The question comes to the surface: How can the God who sees all have anything to regret?

When people feel regret, it usually follows a misstep—a missed opportunity, a failure, or a choice that brought unintended pain. There is a sting in wishing we could rewind time, fix what went wrong, or avoid hurting someone. **The repent/regret experienced** <u>by God</u> in **Genesis 6:6** <u>does not fit easily into this box</u>. God's foreknowledge and perfect vision mean He is not surprised; nothing catches Him off guard. Ancient interpreters and thoughtful readers wonder whether regret in God signals some kind of weakness or limitation. But this way of thinking overlooks the depth of sorrow that can coexist with total awareness. **God's regret/repent points to a sorrowful engagement with the world**—a heartbreak not because He was mistaken, but because He is personally invested in the people He created. This moment reveals a divine willingness to feel deeply for creation and stands as a powerful example of **God's relational character**. When the text says God's *"heart was filled with pain,"* it shows a creator who cares so much that human brokenness genuinely matters to Him. (*Divine Regret: Understanding God's Grief over Saul's Rejection*, 2025).

This is not the only time scripture reveals God's emotions. **God rejoices over His people**, as in **Zephaniah 3:17**, and He weeps in the person of Jesus at Lazarus's tomb in **John 11:35**. Passages throughout the Hebrew Bible and New Testament describe God as loving, angry, jealous, or compassionate. These emotions always reflect God's unwavering moral vision and love, not a loss of control or confusion. The regret in Genesis 6:6, then, should not be confusion on God's part about the future or a sign He made a mistake. Instead, it points to His willingness to be present with people in real pain and disappointment, refusing to be a cold, distant observer.

Seeing divine regret as sorrowful investment helps readers grasp God's role as a caring parent or committed friend. Imagine a parent watching their child make poor choices. The parent may know the outcome, may even have warned the child, yet still feels pain and disappointment as they see the consequences unfold. Yet these feelings do not spring from not knowing, but from love—the kind of love that aches when someone you care for strays. When Genesis portrays God as grieving, it offers a window into God's passionate commitment. Human actions impact the divine-human relationship, not because God is at our mercy, but because **He set up creation to be a true relationship**, giving space for love, faithfulness, or betrayal to matter.

This understanding adds rich meaning to doctrines about God's compassion. God is not indifferent to the world's suffering or to people's failures. Divine regret/repent calls attention to God's hope for human flourishing, His moral standards, and His willingness to enter into the mess with creation. It does not diminish God's power or knowledge; instead, it lifts up the sort of **powerful empathy** that transforms how we pray, worship, and approach God. God's openness to relational joy and pain means that, even when humanity chooses selfishness or violence, the story is not closed. **Divine repent/regret is paired with divine patience**. The flood narrative does not only end in judgment but also in a promise—God's sorrow is not a barrier to future restoration.

Readers can respond to these ideas by asking how their choices shape their own relationship with God. If divine regret means God's heart aches over injustice or brokenness, what does that say about the value He places on human decisions? People may pause and ask: Do my choices bring joy to God's heart, or pain? How can I align my life in ways that reflect God's own desires for me? By recognizing God's emotional investment, faith becomes more than a distant belief—it takes on the intimacy of a relationship where one's actions genuinely matter.

By exploring regret in this way, the text not only gives a sense of God's closeness, but also prepares the way to consider how language about **God's repentance or regret <u>explores</u> even deeper <u>mysteries</u>**. If God can express sorrow, what does it mean for scripture to speak of God "repenting"? These questions invite readers onward into greater reflection, sustaining the sense of wonder sparked by the first glimpse of divine regret.

POSSIBILITY OF INTERPRETATION 2:

Understanding Divine Repentance: Theological Insights

Human stories about regret almost always involve learning, changing direction, or recognizing a mistake. **Genesis 6:6-7** *features an account of God's "regret" or "repentance"* regarding the creation of humanity. While this language reflects a **powerful sense of loss and grief**, the Bible never suggests that God learns the way people do, makes blunders, or fails to foresee the outcome of His actions. The idea of God repenting cannot mean that God lacked wisdom or misunderstood consequences. Instead, the narrative paints God as genuinely sorrowful over the violence and wickedness that fill the earth. **The word "repentance"** helps readers feel the seriousness of the situation, bringing them into the emotional heart of the biblical story.

Human repentance often involves a humble admission and a call for forgiveness, because people get things wrong or break relationships. **God's "repentance" presented in Genesis 6:6-7 is not an admission of fault**. The passage carefully points to a God who loves His creation so much that He willingly expresses sorrow when humanity falls into ruin. The language allows us to enter into God's response, showing that divine grief is real and active. When the Bible says God "regrets" or "repents," it does not describe a shift in divine character. Instead, <u>it describes a living God interacting with the consequences of human rebellion, heartbreak</u>, and violence. These moments offer a window into God's patience and investment in what He has made.

These questions invite a deeper theological conversation. When readers see words like "repentance" or "grief" used for God, some interpret them anthropopathically. This approach recognizes that **the Bible sometimes gives God human-like feelings and qualities** <u>to help people understand</u> His inner life. Biblical writers use human language so readers can catch glimpses of who God is, **even though God's essence** **is far richer and more mysterious**. For example, the same scriptures talk about God's "anger," "laughter," or "jealousy." These terms don't limit God to human moods but serve as pictures that draw readers closer to God's heart.

Another approach highlights that biblical stories sometimes show God responding dynamically to people's choices. In these passages, God "relents" or turns away from judgment after people change their ways or pray for mercy. **The book of Jonah chapter 3: verse 10; gives a vivid picture**: The people of Nineveh hear God's warning and turn from evil. **God "repented"** <u>of the planned disaster</u> – (Bible-KJV), not because He is capricious, but because He always honors humanity's true repentance and faith. In Exodus 32:14 (KJV), Moses pleads for Israel after their rebellion, and God holds back (or repented of) the destruction. Both stories show that God's interaction with His world is real and unfolds as people respond. These portrayals spark important questions about whether God's will can truly change, or if the Bible simply shows God's actions from a human perspective.

At the root of these discussions stands the <u>Creator-creature</u> distinction. God's thoughts, motives, and actions always rise above the limits of human experience. While humans must respond to new information, God knows and sees everything at once. **Divine "repentance"** <u>is not an admission of mistake</u> but a faithful response to the unfolding story of creation—a story in which humans are invited to participate. God's sovereignty and humanity's freedom meet in these accounts. Scripture holds the tension between God's sure purpose and His response to human choices. God's openness in these passages doesn't threaten His power; it affirms His commitment to authentic relationship with people.

For those grappling with these questions, several guiding principles can help shape faith and action. When the Bible shows **God grieving** over sin, it challenges everyone to turn away from patterns that sabotage relationships. <u>God's willingness to feel pain over human wrongdoing</u> calls people to honest self-examination and to make changes that lead toward healing and renewal. For instance, a person who has lied and hurt someone may, after recognizing the consequences, feel regret and seek reconciliation. **God's "repentance" in Genesis 6:6 is not weakness**—it is an invitation for people to be honest, to grieve what is broken, and to rebuild through love and humility.

Church communities find hope in the idea that God's heart is moved by their prayers and actions. In times of sadness or failure, this picture offers comfort: God takes sin and redemption seriously and longs to see restoration more than judgment. Recognizing that God's greatest desire is to repair and not destroy, people are encouraged to act boldly, seek forgiveness, reach out to others, and trust God's power to transform brokenness into new beginnings.

Summary & Reflection of this Topic

Now that we have unpacked the profound meaning behind divine **Repent/regret**, we can approach Scripture with a deeper appreciation for **God's emotional involvement in our world** and <u>His longing for genuine relationship with humanity</u>. Recognizing that **God's sorrow is not a flaw** but a <u>powerful sign of</u> **care** and as consequence, this invites us to reflect on how our choices affect this sacred connection. Armed with this understanding, young adults, Bible study groups, and curious readers alike are encouraged to engage more fully with the biblical text, asking meaningful questions and embracing the mystery of a God who grieves, hopes, and patiently waits for restoration. **This new perspective** opens the door to richer discussions about faith, challenges us to align our lives with <u>God's desires</u>, and prepares us to explore further theological insights into God's dynamic presence throughout Holy Scripture.

Reference List of Chapter 9

Biblical Reference:

Genesis 6:6-7 *"And it 'repented' LORD that he had made man on the earth, and it grieved at his heart."*
*7 And **The LORD said**, … … for '**it repenteth me**' **that I** have made them.".* – (Bible) King James Version.

Other Referebces:

Agana-Nsiire Agana. (2018). *A Theological Reflection on the Relationship Between Divine Omniscience and Human Free Will*. Thesis.

AC21DOJ.org. (2024). Ac21doj.org.

Divine Regret: Understanding God's Grief Over Saul's Rejection. (2025). Prezi.com.

Duby. (2018). *"For I Am God, Not a Man."* Journal of Theological Interpretation.

PART 3:

Moment of

Imminent Resolution

Chapter 10:

Strange

Singularity (Who?)

Genesis 6:8-9

*"8 But <u>Noah found grace in the eyes of the LORD</u>. 9 These are the generations of Noah: **<u>Noah was a just man and perfect in his generations</u>**, and <u>Noah walked with God</u>".* – (Bible – K.J.V.).

Only One Person in the Entire Planet living in Justice!

"Noah was a **righteous man**, <u>blameless among the people of his time,</u> *and he walked faithfully with God."* – **Genesis 6:8-9**. (Bible – N.I.V.) These words from Genesis might seem simple at first, but they carry a weight that echoes through history. **Imagine living in a world where goodness is so rare** that <u>only one person</u> stands firm in what is right. What does it mean to be truly **just** when everything around you seems broken? How does **one person's faithfulness** hold up <u>against a culture filled with violence and corruption</u>?

This chapter invites you to step into Noah's world, a place filled with <u>challenges both seen and unseen</u>. It asks questions about courage, integrity, and the cost of standing apart. When no one else chooses **the path of justice**, what drives someone to keep walking it anyway? And what impact can that loyalty have on those closest to them—and beyond? As you read, consider your own choices and the quiet strength it takes <u>to live with purpose</u>, **even when it means standing alone**.

José E. Espinoza

POSSIBILITY OF INTERPRETATION 1:

Context of Noah's Justice/Righteousness

The ancient world in Genesis appears torn apart by patterns of evil and unchecked violence, a place where the difference between right and wrong are only shadows. Against this bleak landscape, **Noah stands alone**. His righteousness is not casual; it is a stark contrast to the culture of deceit, cruelty, and moral decay surrounding him. God's selection of Noah is purposeful. The biblical record zeroes in on Noah's life, showing him as **a rare instance** of someone who clings to decency while the world chooses chaos. In one of the most recognized passages, Genesis highlights: *"Noah found grace in the eyes of the Lord...Noah was a righteous man, blameless among the people of his time, and he walked faithfully with God"* (**Genesis 6:8-9**). These words reveal the foundation for God's decision—Noah's **pursuit of justice** and **obedience** distinguished him.

The difference between Noah and his generation is illustrated not only in actions but in attitudes. While others yielded to corruption, driven by selfish gain and disregard for life, Noah's focus on **living rightly** sets him apart. He is not perfect, but resolved in his faithfulness, and that is the trait **God recognizes**. While the violence outside his household roared louder each day, Noah worked steadily on his task, undistracted by the ridicule or skepticism of his contemporaries. Spiritual courage required him to look beyond his own survival, taking hold of an assignment that would extend God's mercy to his family and the broader animal kingdom.

This commitment to faith and integrity is not a private matter. The scope of Noah's influence reaches into his closest relationships. Everything about the ark project required sustained team effort, especially from family members who may have wrestled with doubt themselves. Noah, through his actions and daily example, shaped the home's climate. **Leadership here is evident** not only in directive roles—building, gathering, planning—but in the consistency of character displayed under pressure. His sons, Shem, Ham, and Japheth, and their wives, followed him into a future that seemed outrageous to others. Though the text focuses squarely on Noah, family participation suggests <u>his integrity and trust in God spread through his household</u> and held them together through an episode that shattered every sense of normalcy.

The wider world **in Noah's day** is a warning, a picture of the outcomes when ethical boundaries dissolve. <u>Genesis paints a society where violence</u>, betrayal, and disregard for basic decency have normalized. The power of Noah's example is in his quiet resistance, his everyday choices that mark him as different. Readers then and now can picture themselves alongside him, deciding whether to conform or to hold on to what is right.

This solitary stance is not empty isolation; it creates a foundation for obedience and righteousness. The focus on **one "just" man** is both sobering and hopeful. In a world that had lost its bearings, one person's choice reshaped human history. The post-flood covenant underscores that **righteous living is not irrelevant**, <u>even when rare</u>. Noah's life teaches that the legacy of faith is both immediate—his family's rescue—and ongoing, setting an example for future generations about the costs and rewards of standing firm in what is right.

The attention drawn to Noah as **the sole "just" one** hints at deeper questions about his peers. If he alone is righteous, what about others? Was there no one else, or did something unique allow him to persevere? Thinking about the reasons for spiritual isolation leads to further reflection on justice and mercy, preparing for a closer study into why the biblical narrative remains silent on other figures and **what it means to be just** <u>in God's sight</u>. Noah's life remains a guidepost, his faith echoing into centuries where individuals must weigh similar choices about conformity, courage, and legacy.

POSSIBILITY OF INTERPRETATION 2:

Question of Other Righteous Descendants; What Happened?

Noah stands out in Genesis, not just because of his actions, but by the stark absence of anyone else described as righteous. The world around him teems with corruption, yet **Genesis says nothing about other men or women** <u>following God's ways</u>. This silence isn't accidental. It pushes readers to face the harsh spiritual health of Noah's day and to ask: <u>what does it really mean</u> **to be called a just man among millions**? This was a landscape more than crowded—it was noisy with invention, desire, and violence, but **strangely** calm and quiet about **faithfulness** <u>beyond one solitary figure</u>.

Genesis 6:8-9 gives us the phrase, *"Noah was <u>a just man</u> and perfect in his generations; and Noah walked with God."* **The word "just"** here is not a throwaway description. When the text says ***"just man,"*** it means <u>someone whose choices run against the grain</u>, **not because of inherited goodness**, but deliberate living. To be righteous in those days didn't just mean following rules well. It meant seeing what nobody else saw, hearing what everyone else ignored, and <u>choosing</u>

differently every day. Noah's difference wasn't genetic. He stood alone because nobody else decided to stand with him.

Scripture's silence about other contenders for righteousness raises a sharp question—**were there truly no others?** Maybe some shrank back, unwilling to pay the price of friendship with God. The cost of **"walking with God"** wasn't light. In a world driven by speed, appetite, and controversy, Noah's way was slower and costly. To "walk with God" meant risking disconnection from family, friends, and public acceptance, cutting oneself out just as surely as one is called in. The story tells us nothing of small, hidden flickers of faith elsewhere. **It is as if the world's spiritual landscape had dried out**, leaving only one small patch of green.

The absence of other named righteous people points the spotlight directly at Noah. Faith does not automatically root itself in a family, tribe, or generation. It cannot be passed down like heirlooms. **Each person stands free to choose alignment with God**, or not. In practical terms, Genesis 5:30 remarks that Noah had brothers and sisters, and (assuming) uncles, cousins, (Genesis 5:26) and even/maybe friends. Yet the text only calls his name. This underlines that righteousness is more than membership. It rests on decision and resolve. In a crumbling world, everyone faces moments where they could step toward God but often do not.

Genesis drops hints about why faith may have been so rare. The descendants of Adam and Eve had grown numerous. With their numbers came advances, stories, and even technology—ancient knowledge of metals and 'magic', legends (according to possibly interpretations) say, passed on by rogue beings (*Inthedaysofnoah*, 2024). With all this, the temptation to follow the crowd grew louder. The cost of being different increased. Isolation waits for anyone refusing to give in to the tide. **Noah** woke up each morning to a world that found him **strange,** stubborn, or even wrong for his convictions.

Take the idea of righteousness as a choice. Imagine someone else living at that time, noticing the mess rising all around—the violence, the corruption, the daily side-eyed glances at **Noah and his strange ways**. Maybe they wondered privately if he was right. Maybe they questioned their own hearts. But for whatever reason—fear, desire for belonging, disbelief—it stayed as just that, a private wondering. The text shows that almost everyone moved with the current. **Noah's courage and valor was not only doing right,** but doing it when nobody would join him.

Modern readers can find themselves in similar places. Peer pressure is old as time. The struggle to live by faith when the world rolls its eyes or closes its ears—this is not ancient history. People face moments where standing up for truth, honesty, justice, or kindness means standing apart. Noah's story shouts that faith becomes real only when it is costly and public.

This focus on one man asks hard questions. **Is righteousness rare** because it is hard, or because it is lonely? Does God single out those who are made for this kind of solitude, or is every one of us invited to take that uncomfortable step toward justice, even if nobody follows?

Genesis leaves a gap where other names might appear, and it means something that the gap stayed empty.

Bible study groups, young adults or seekers wrestling with doubt, can dig deeper into these silent spaces. Where are the missed chances for redemption? What would it look like if more than one person risked faith? In every age, the story of **Noah invites us** to ask whether small choices matter in a vast, noisy world. It leaves everyone with another chance to be counted, <u>to walk justly in whichever world we find ourselves</u>, even if we must do it alone.

Summary & Reflection of this Topic

Now that we have seen how **Noah's Justice/righteousness stood firm** <u>in a world filled with wrongdoing</u> and silence from others, we can recognize the powerful example he sets for us today. His story challenges us to consider what **it means to live faithfully when those around us choose a different path**, reminding us that true righteousness is a choice made daily, <u>often in solitude and opposition</u>. As we reflect on Noah's courage, valor and commitment, we are invited to step forward with our own **acts of faith and justice**, knowing that even one person's decision can shape the course of history and inspire generations to come. This chapter leaves us with a clear message: standing for what is right may be difficult and lonely, but it is also where change begins, and where hope lives—calling each of us to walk with integrity in whatever world we face.

Reference List of Chapter 10

Biblical reference:

Genesis 6:8-9. *"But Noah found grace in the eyes of the LORD. 9 These are the generations of Noah:* **Noah was _a just man_ and perfect _in his generations_***, and Noah walked with God".* – King James Version of **the Bible**

Other References:

Apocalypse | BillMoyers.com. (2015, June 25). BillMoyers.com.

Alexander, T. D. (n.d.). *Genesis.* The Gospel Coalition.

Inthedaysofnoah. (2024). Inthedaysofnoah.

Yndyiago. (2023, December 21). *In-Depth Bible Study Notes on Genesis Chapters 6-10.* Lemon8.

Chapter 11:

Strange

"God's Decision"...

Genesis 6:13

*"So God said to Noah, **I have decided to destroy all** living creatures, for they have filled the earth with violence. Yes, I will wipe them all out along with the earth!" – NLT (Bible).*

Before The Flood; Genesis 5-7
127

Determination <u>to Destroy It All</u> in Genesis 6:13

What does it mean when <u>a God who is known for love</u> and mercy **decides to wipe out nearly all life on earth**? This question has puzzled readers for centuries, challenging the way we understand justice, forgiveness, and the consequences of human choices. Imagine a world so deeply broken that every part of life—from people's hearts to the animals and land itself—is marred by corruption and violence. What kind of failure leads to such a dramatic decision? And how can a Creator, patient beyond measure, reach a point where **destruction becomes necessary**? These unsettling questions invite us to look closely at an ancient story that goes far beyond straightforward punishment. It asks us to consider the nature of moral decay, the limits of patience, and the complex balance between judgment and hope. In this chapter, we explore a **divine determination** that changed everything and set the stage for renewal, revealing layers of meaning that go deeper than we might expect.

POSSIBILITY OF INTERPRETATION 1:

Understanding <u>Total Corruption</u> and God's Patience

Genesis 6:13

*"I have determined to make an end of **<u>all flesh</u>**,"*… - E.S.V.

The phrase *"all flesh had corrupted its way on the earth"* in **Genesis 6:12** points to a collapse more sweeping than mere physical decay or individual misdeeds. In the Hebrew Bible, **"flesh"** goes beyond muscle and bone to include **the whole of living existence**—moral, spiritual, personal, and even the social ties that define human life. To say **"all flesh" was corrupted** <u>shows that society, not only individuals,</u> had steered itself away from God's purpose. The text carries the sense of **moral rot** and a <u>hardening of the human will against God's intended order.</u> Instead of community built on faithfulness and care, violence and self-interest filled the world, signaling the loss of mutual responsibility. **Genesis 6:11** sums it up simply: *"Now the earth was corrupt in God's sight, and the earth was filled with violence."* Here, "corrupt" means broken at the core, while "violence" signals a breakdown of trust and justice where the strong exploit the weak and peace cannot last.

The spread of corruption was not a chain of isolated bad choices, but a deep-rooted way of life that infected every region and relationship. Families no longer relied on trust, communities fractured, and leaders could not be counted on for justice. Shared stories and wisdom, once passed down to bind people together, were lost or twisted. As described in writings from the Second Temple period, the chaos and cruelty of this age grew as supernatural rebellion escalated, and humanity itself seemed on the verge of becoming unrecognizable. <u>Some traditions tied this to the presence of the Nephilim</u>, 'mysterious figures' whose actions marked the cost of turning away from God. Their violence, along with the spread of lawlessness, erased the boundaries between the human and the wild, the sacred and the profane.

What makes "all flesh" even more haunting is that "flesh" here 'includes animals'. Genesis makes clear that the animals' fate was bound to humanity's choices. God says to Noah, *"I will destroy them with the earth"* (**Genesis 6:13**). This is not a statement about animals having rebelled in a human sense. Instead, it shows how intertwined life is, how human failure can bring suffering and loss to the whole creation. The world's balance—relationships between people, land, and the rest of nature—collapsed once human beings quit living for anything higher than themselves. The world became a place where nothing and no one could thrive. This reminds us that in real life, when communities lose their way, the results ripple outward— ecological destruction, lost trust, neighbors turning suspicious or hostile, innocence overrun by harm and fear.

The description in Genesis is not about a harsh or impulsive act from God. The buildup to judgment reveals time, warning, and the chance for change. Noah stands as the lone example of faith and obedience, *"blameless in his generation"*. This "blamelessness" may mean more than moral uprightness—it could suggest, as some suggest, that Noah's family was not swept up in either the moral or "genetic" corruption associated with the Nephilim. One of the strongest (possible) Interpretations is that; **God's decision to bring the Flood** comes only after a long, patient wait, **with 120 years between the first warning and the actual judgment**. During that time, (many academic scholars believe) Noah "preached righteousness," offering mercy and a way back. **Only when it was clear that no one would choose change** did the judgment fall. In this light, **God's act is not blind wrath** but the necessary decision to halt a world so damaged it cannot heal itself.

Even here, the story points forward. The destruction is not just about erasing what is broken, but about opening space for something new. Noah, his family, and the animals on the ark are set aside—a **remnant kept alive through disaster**, proof of God's refusal to completely abandon creation. This sets up the hope that **judgment need not be the end**. The story prepares readers to look for ways that new beginnings can follow even after everything falls apart. God's ongoing relationship with the survivors hints at mercy that can work out renewal, even from the ruins of "all flesh" corrupted.

José E. Espinoza

POSSIBILITY OF INTERPERTATION 2:

Nature of Corrupted Flesh and Hope in Redemption

As corruption set in, the world grew harder, noisier, more chaotic. The normalization of violence is evident: people thought nothing of harming their neighbors if it meant getting ahead. Kindness and generosity became rare, like small flowers in a battered field. Competition and suspicion ran high, dividing people who might once have cared for one another. The earth itself bore the marks of this distortion. **According to some interpretations**, even the animals began to act in ways they were never meant to—once peaceful creatures (possibly) turning predatory or strange, echoing the unrest of the human world. Through this lens, even creation's natural rhythms broke down, and the peaceful order God had made collapsed. When God speaks of "all flesh" being corrupt, the vision is of a world where the boundaries between human and animal chaos start to blur, with the whole system groaning for a relief.

God's decision to judge "all flesh" was not just about punishing people for breaking moral rules. The harm went deeper. **The story suggests creation itself became warped by ongoing evil**. Animals, plants, the land—nothing escaped the touch of sin. Violence spilled over into every part of daily life. People (according to some possibilities of interpretations), committed acts of bloodlust, theft, and deceit, and these behaviors became common. Home was no longer a safe place. Families were torn apart by selfishness, children were neglected or even abused, and parents abandoned the task of guiding their sons and daughters toward goodness. Social gatherings failed to produce trust or celebration; instead, they became hotbeds for plotting and wrongdoing. Even the routines of planting, harvesting, traveling—basic actions that used to connect humans to one another and to creation—no longer carried meaning or safety.

Judgment arrives in this story <u>because anything less would have allowed evil to keep spreading</u>, pulling everything further from hope. God's justice meets the world not out of spite, but as the only possible response when every structure meant for good unravels. **The world did not fall overnight**; <u>the rot set in over generations</u>, as each person chose themselves over the well-being of others. The result? An earth brimming with violence, suspicion, and pain. Chaos had to be answered with something mighty enough to clear the wreckage, making space for something new. **The flood signals a reset**—<u>not a final end</u>, but a determined act meant to stop ruin from becoming permanent.

Yet within this dark valley, the text places subtle threads of hope. **God's decision to save Noah and the animals** is a <u>sign that restoration lies beyond judgment</u>. Even as the waters rise, the promise is there—a plan to renew the earth and begin again. Noah's preservation is not random. The narrative points to him as a seed of faithfulness and transformation. The God who brings the storm also crafts a new promise, committing not only to humanity, but to every creature. The covenant after the flood includes animals and the earth itself, showing that mercy and the chance for a new beginning reach further than punishment alone. Suffering, in this light, does not close the book on hope. Instead, it clears space so that something pure and right can take root—a reminder that, even amid chaos and collapse, **God's story continues moving toward redemption** for all creation.

Summary & Reflection of this Topic

Now that we understand the deep corruption described in the flood story and God's patient warning before judgment, we can see this event not simply as an end but as a powerful **call to reflection** and <u>renewal</u>. It challenges us to think about how choices affect not just individuals but whole communities and creation itself, reminding us of the importance of living with faithfulness, care, and justice. This ancient narrative invites young readers and study groups alike to explore difficult questions about sin, mercy, and hope, encouraging us to look beyond destruction toward the possibility of new beginnings. By grappling with these themes, we open ourselves to a richer understanding of God's justice—**not as harsh punishment**, <u>but as a necessary step toward healing</u> a broken world, and ultimately, toward redemption for all life.

Reference List of Chapter 11

Biblical reference:

Genesis 6:13 *"So God said to Noah, **I have decided to destroy all** living creatures...'"* – *New Living Translation of **the Bible***

Other References:

Finnegan, S. (2022, March 26). *Are we born with a morally corrupt nature? (Sin 2)*. Restitutio.

Mooney, J. (2023, August 13). *Genesis 6 Reimagined: Loren Stuckenbruck on Angels, Giants, and Judgment - Chasing the Giants*. Chasing the Giants.

Nicolaides, S. G., & Nicolaides, A. G. (2024, August 18). *Divine Law and Animal Rights: Ethical and Legal Perspectives in the Old and New Testaments*. Pharos Journal of Theology; AfricaJournals.

Was God Unjust in Sending the Flood? (2025, January 30). Tom's Theology Blog.

Chapter 12:

Mystery of

"The Wood to Make de Ark" (?)

Genesis 6:14

"Make yourself an ark of __gopher wood__. Make rooms in the ark, and cover it inside and out with pitch". – ESV (Bible)

Strange Uncertain Tree

Did you know the Bible mentions a type of wood called 'gopher' only once? I had never paused to wonder about it before—why that specific wood? What made it so special that Noah's Ark was built from **such specific tree**? The question seemed simple at first but soon opened up a deeper puzzle tied to **ancient trees**, <u>forgotten forests</u>, and <u>mysteries hidden within Scripture</u>.

Many people read through Genesis without noticing this unusual word, yet **its rarity** invites us to look beyond the surface. It points to a world very different from our own, where certain kinds of wood held meanings we no longer fully understand. Over centuries, scholars and believers alike have tried to uncover what "gopher wood" really meant, and in doing so, they've found connections to history, faith, nature, and hope.

This mystery also encourages us to think about how the natural world has changed—from vast, rich forests that may have covered the earth before the flood, to the altered landscapes that followed. It raises questions about how humanity relates to creation and what we might learn by remembering what was lost.

As we begin this exploration, consider how one small, puzzling phrase can open a window into an ancient world filled with life and meaning. It challenges us to look carefully, to ask questions, and to listen for lessons not only about a specific kind of wood but about trust, stewardship, and the stories woven through time.

POSSIBILITY OF INTERPRETATION 1:

Exploring <u>Gopher Wood</u>'s Significance and Symbolism

Most casual readers of Genesis pass over the phrase "ark of gopher wood" in **Genesis 6:14** without pausing, but this phrase opens a door to a bigger world of questions. The word "gopher" appears just once in the entire Hebrew Bible—its uniqueness marks it as a kind of ancient riddle. Scholars, translators, and commentators have puzzled over its meaning for generations. For Moses and his first audience, **"gopher wood"** <u>was likely a known term</u> and carried its own weight, **yet for later readers**, it **stands out as <u>an enigma</u>** that hints at lost knowledge of ancient trees and practices.

Several competing theories about gopher wood's identity have surfaced. One <u>prominent suggestion links it (possibly)</u> **to cypress**, a wood famous in the ancient world for its longevity and resistance to decay. <u>Cypress wood</u>, for instance, played a crucial role in building temples, ships, and coffins in old Mediterranean civilizations, prized for surviving centuries without rotting or falling prey to insects. **Cedar** <u>is another (possibly) candidate</u>. In Lebanon, cedar trees were long regarded as symbols of prosperity and protection, and their wood furnished palaces, shrines, and ships throughout the ancient Near

3

East. Both woods, whether cypress or cedar, would have been well suited to the ark's size and intended use—durable enough to withstand months of rain and a floating menagerie.

Yet the theory that gopher wood was an extinct species draws from the text's mystery rather than from familiar woods. <u>If Noah used a tree now lost to time</u>, this points toward a **pre-flood environment rich in biodiversity**, <u>with unique forests now erased by the Flood itself</u>. The loss of such a tree would reflect the dramatic ecological changes between the antediluvian and post-flood worlds—a puzzle that naturally draws in readers curious about the vanished landscapes of Genesis. Imagining gopher wood as the remnant of a lost creation suggests Genesis is not just an account of catastrophic judgment and rescue but a narrative shadowed by threads of environmental memory.

Symbolically, **gopher wood's obscurity** has inspired many reflections on its role in the biblical story. <u>**God gave Noah detailed instructions** for building an unprecedented structure</u>, demanding trust in both materials and method. **Choosing a wood** everyone could recognize would have made the account matter-of-fact; instead, the narrative chooses the unknown, inviting thoughtful exploration. Gopher wood becomes a symbol of obedience, requiring Noah to act on faith and follow directions without knowing every answer—mirroring the walk of faith for all who trust in divine command over certainty.

The debate over gopher wood's true nature also invites readers to reflect on humanity's relationship with nature. Interpreters have found in its enigma a metaphor: using rare or mysterious resources wisely, stewarding creation with care, and following God's directions instead of relying on human knowledge alone. This theme of stewardship can prompt lively discussion about responsibility, gratitude, and humility in the face of both abundance and mystery.

Jewish and Christian sources have not been content to accept gopher wood as simply unknown. Rabbinic traditions imagined it as a miraculous wood grown for God's purposes alone; medieval commentaries collected legends, linguistic guesses, and even comparisons with other biblical trees. Christian commentators have written about obedience, endurance, or the lost knowledge that gopher wood suggests. The ongoing debate has become a collaboration across time, with each new suggestion, comparison, or legend keeping the question alive.

Gopher wood, then, stands not only as a practical building material but as a signpost pointing to larger questions. Its puzzle captures the lost richness of the pre-flood forests, calling readers to picture a world where extraordinary trees shaped survival and meaning. **How did those forests look?** What knowledge faded when the floodwaters rose? The search for answers draws us from the puzzle of one word to a vision of a vanished, ancient world whose lessons reach far beyond the ark's planks.

POSSIBILITY OF INTERPRETATION 2:

Examining Pre- and Post-Flood Forest Ecosystems

Scholars and readers have long **wondered about Gopher wood's** qualities and its <u>mysterious disappearance</u> from human memory. The loss of its physical details opens the door to a bigger question: **what kind of forests and plants once filled the landscape**, <u>producing a wood worthy of Noah's Ark</u>? The early chapters of Genesis hint at a world teeming with life and resources. Drawing on both the biblical text and ideas from those who study these ancient times, one can picture an earth with huge stretches of wild forests, each more vibrant than what we see today.

Some suggest the <u>pre-flood climate was (possibly) gentle and even, without the sharp seasons found in many places now</u>. Imagine forests that never faced frost or endless droughts—a setting where trees could grow old and large, stretching their branches without fear of sudden cold or heat waves. **In these imagined forests**, trees stood in grand clusters alongside rich undergrowth and ferns, much like the thickest rainforests but perhaps even more diverse. The air may have been heavy with moisture, encouraging moss, towering plants, and trees loaded with fruit or fragrant woods. **Gopher wood may have come**

from a tree lost to time, <u>gone with the flood</u> and the forests erased beneath the waters.

It's possible these forests included many trees now only known as fossils or distant relatives. **Old trunk imprints in rock** <u>sometimes reveal plants much different from those growing today</u>. Perhaps Gopher wood's source tree shared its world with giant calamitous trees, dense thickets of cycads, or palms thicker than any found now. Some believe this era's forests rivaled the Amazon or the great redwood groves—untouched, hushing with hidden life, and offering endless types of wood for people to use.

When the flood rose, its waters would have swept aside this thriving world in a matter of weeks. Entire forests were ripped up, buried, or washed away, leaving behind sediment and chaos. Long stretches of tree life winked out. **The destruction was not only about the water's force**; <u>it was a **new climate**</u>, too. 'After the flood, the sky (possibly) changed. Seasons appeared, and harsh cold and blistering heat shaped what could grow. <u>Trees not built for these shifts vanished,</u> and <u>only those able to adapt returned</u>. If Gopher wood's tree was one of those unable to survive, its story ends in the mud below the floodwaters.

Imagining the post-flood world, the forests must have seemed thin and uncertain to Noah's family. Instead of picking from endless supplies of building materials, people now had to search harder, settle for whatever survived, and learn new ways to manage what they found. Oak and cedar, pine and acacia—familiar trees for later generations—might have only filled parts of the landscape, much less impressive in number and size than before. The world's treasures became memories, stories passed down, or mysteries like the 'lost Gopher wood'.

For the people living before the flood, life in such a world meant never worrying about finding resources. With many trees and plants available, shelter, food, and tools could be made with ease. The forests would have offered shade from the gentle sun and rooms carved out in the wild for family and work. Exploring these woods, ancient families gathered fruit, cut strong beams, and shaped homes from what they found right outside their doors. This abundance likely shaped attitudes toward the land—taking only what was needed and living in peace with nature's gifts.

Yet after the flood, every stick of timber and each handful of food began to matter more. Losing access to these forests became a lesson in loss and a call to remember what had once been possible. The story of the Ark, built with the last of a legendary wood, stands as a reminder: resources are not endless. Each time the Bible mentions a powerful tree or a sacred forest—the tree of life, the cedars of Lebanon, or the fig trees shading a prophet—it echoes that lost abundance. Trees become symbols for both provision and responsibility.

This memory invites today's readers of Genesis to think about stewardship. If the world's treasures can vanish, it matters how they are used. The Ark's **Gopher wood, now a mystery**, urges care and respect for what still grows. Ancient forests, once celebrated for their beauty and usefulness, leave behind a message written in stories and lost names: abundance gives way to scarcity, and the wise care for the earth as a trust, not just a resource.

Summary & Reflection of this Topic

Now that we have explored **the mystery of gopher wood** and its place in the pre-flood world, we can see how this single, puzzling detail opens up a richer understanding of humanity's relationship with nature and faith. The story of the ark challenges us to think about the lost forests and resources that once supported life, reminding us that God's instructions often require trust beyond what we fully understand. As we reflect on the vanished trees and **changing ecosystems**, we are invited to consider our own role as stewards of creation, valuing what remains and caring for it wisely. This journey through ancient wood and forgotten forests encourages deeper questions and discussions, helping us uncover new meaning in familiar texts and inspiring faith that embraces both **mystery** and responsibility.

Reference List of Chapter 12

Biblical reference:

Genesis 6:14 *"Make yourself an **ark of <u>Gopher</u>**/Cypress wood; make rooms in it"* – English Standard Version of the **Bible**

Other References:

Chaffey, D. T. (2020, October 7). *Gopher Wood: The Mystery of the Ark's Timber.* Answers in Genesis; Answers In Genesis.

House, C. P. (2025, August 28). *Historical and Biblical Background of Genesis 6–8: Noah's Ark, the Flood, and God's Covenant - Updated American Standard Version.* Updated American Standard Version.

José E. Espinoza

Chapter 13:

Mysterious

"4 Women" (Whom?)

Genesis 6:18

*"... Your **wife**, and your sons' **wives**..." – NAS (Bible)*

'4 Flood female Survivals', '<u>Matriarchs</u> of the rest of Humanity'; No Names!

When we think of the story of Noah's Ark, our minds often focus on the giant boat, the animals boarding two by two, and the flood that wiped out nearly all life on earth. Yet, amid this dramatic tale, certain figures stand quietly in the background—**<u>4 women whose names are never spoken</u>** but whose presence is essential. <u>Noah's wife</u> and <u>the wives of his three sons</u> **remain unnamed in the Bible**, <u>their identities a mystery</u> wrapped in silence. While the men receive detailed genealogies and personal encounters with God, <u>these women are introduced only by their roles</u>. Their stories are left untold, yet they play a crucial part in what comes after the flood: the survival and rebuilding of humanity.

This chapter explores the **significance of these unnamed women** in **Genesis 6:18**. We will examine why their anonymity matters, what it reveals about the culture and theology of the time, and how it invites us to consider the hidden influences behind history's great moments. By looking closely at their possible backgrounds and the meanings scholars have proposed, this discussion opens up new ways to think about faith, <u>legacy, and human complexity</u>. **These silent women** challenge us to see <u>beyond names and titles</u>, reminding us that sometimes the most important stories are those told in quiet strength and faithful endurance.

POSSIBILITY OF INTERPRETATION 1:

Exploring the Unnamed Women and Their Impact

The few verses in Genesis that mention Noah's wife and the wives of his sons give only the barest details, yet these unnamed women stand at a pivotal moment in history. When the floodwaters rise and all life outside the ark perishes, it is these four women—Noah's wife, and the three wives of Shem, Ham, and Japheth—who, alongside their husbands, become **the sole surviving ancestors** of all future people. Their presence is assumed rather than explained; their stories are left out, and their voices are silent in the text. The men in the same narrative receive names, genealogies, and even personal encounters with God. The steadfast anonymity of these women reflects both the cultural reality of ancient Hebrew storytelling and the layered **mystery** that makes speculation about their identities compelling.

Navigating the silence around these figures opens up a field for readers and scholars. In the context of the ancient world, lineage mattered far more through the male line, and biblical texts often highlighted the lives and actions of men. Yet the survival of humanity, as Genesis lays it out, depended just as much on the faithfulness and resilience of these unnamed women. **Genesis 6:18** simply states that

God established a covenant with Noah and told him to bring his wife, his sons, and his sons' wives onto the ark. **These women are never named**, and they do not speak in the text. Their anonymity sits in sharp contrast to the male genealogies threaded through Genesis, emphasizing both their importance and the tension between presence and erasure.

Speculation over their identity runs along a spectrum. One possibility put forward by interpreters links the wives to the righteous descendants of Seth, Adam's third son. Under this theory, these women would serve as representatives of faith and virtue, those who helped ensure the continued spiritual integrity of humankind after the flood. **Alternatively**, some readings (as a possibility of interpretation) connect one or more wives to the mysterious "Daughters of Men" from Genesis 6:2–4—a phrase that, in some traditions, hints at intermingling between the righteous Sethite line and less righteous descendants of Cain. If so, these unions might suggest a blending of spiritual heritage, layering questions about morality, compromise, and God's willingness to select imperfect vessels for world-changing survival. These contrasting theories show how readers are drawn into the creative gap left by the biblical silence, pondering possibilities that shape how the narrative conveys ideas of purity, legacy, and human complexity.

The feature of being unnamed in scripture is not rare. The Bible intersperses its stories of named heroes with characters whose anonymity can be deeply meaningful. For example, **Pharaoh's daughter is not named** (Exodus 2:5-10) when she rescues Moses, the servant girl who tells Naaman about the prophet Elisha (2 Kings 5:2-4) is left nameless, others simply called *"the wife of..."* or "a woman of...." Their anonymity does not mean they lack influence. Instead, it can demonstrate the value of hidden faith and perseverance, suggesting that many of history's true shapers do their work beyond the reach of titles and chronicles. The wives in the flood story fit this pattern. Their actions—gathering animals, supporting their husbands, fostering family strength through a global catastrophe—are not spoken, yet without them, human survival would be impossible. Actions like quiet endurance, supportive labor, and nurturing hope carry a weight that echoes louder than names.

Theologically, a lack of names does more than underline cultural bias. It can underline themes of humility and service that run through biblical thought. Many traditions hold that quiet, faithful work—done for the sake of others rather than personal glory—has God's blessing, and that **the kingdom of God grows** not just through the brave acts of public leaders but also because of steadfast acts of love that remain unseen. Noah's wife and daughters-in-law stand as a symbol for all such faithful but overlooked contributors. Through their anonymity, readers see that God often operates through everyday self-sacrifice and a willingness to serve when history is silent.

The fact that **only their roles**, not their names, are remembered suggests the many layers of influence within a family and a culture. Nurturing children through hardship, passing down teachings, rebuilding community after disaster—these labors have the power to shape history as surely as grand public deeds. **Every future**

generation <u>traces descent back to these unnamed matriarchs</u>, their hidden actions becoming the roots for all that would come. Reflecting on the lives of **Noah's wife and the wives of Shem, Ham, and Japheth** <u>opens the door to wonder about spiritual ancestry</u>, the silent hands that protect and guide society, and the courage it takes to endure faithfully in anonymity.

POSSIBILITY OF INTERPRETATION 2:

Genealogical Connections and Ethical Considerations

Mystery deepens around the unnamed women when their silence meets the shrouded identity of the *"Daughters of Men"* described in Genesis 6. Scripture describes a world ripening with both potential and corruption. The *"sons of God"* and *"daughters of men"* live side by side, their mingling producing children whose presence marks the earth with both renown and violence. The text in Genesis 6:1-4 **hints** (as a possibility of interpretation) at boundary crossing—divine or semi-divine figures intermingling with mortals—and invites much **speculation** about who these women were and what they carried into the generations that followed. Only a short leap connects this idea to questions about Noah's wife and his sons' wives, <u>who step onto the Ark unnamed</u>, yet central to the drama of survival.

Scholars and readers have long noticed the deliberate vagueness around the identity of **Noah's family's wives**. The Genesis account leaves them faceless and <u>origins unrecorded</u>, as if their background were less relevant than their presence at a pivotal moment. Yet their anonymity encourages fresh questions: could these women represent a living thread connecting pre- and post-flood humanity? <u>Some</u>

interpreters **suggest a striking <u>possibility</u>**. Because Genesis presents the "daughters of men" (possibly) as the mothers of the Nephilim and the participants in a union that God views with alarm, the notion that Noah's wife or <u>his sons' wives</u> <u>might come from</u>, or be related to, this group adds rich complexity to the flood story.

This hypothesis prompts a new look at the boundaries between purity and corruption in biblical logic. Early interpreters sometimes drew a strict line between the righteous and the fallen. But embedding a descendant of the "daughters of men" within Noah's family would blur this sharp distinction. God chooses to preserve not just the upright, untouched branch, but a family line that may carry hints of frailty, ambiguity, and even taint. The anonymous women quietly bear both the promise and the risks of such a legacy. They would carry forward not only physical and cultural traits but also the stormy blend of moral struggle and hope.

Biblical genealogies often act as mirrors for debates about redemption and grace. If the wives belonged to a line viewed as tainted, their place on the Ark marks a deliberate act of inclusion. The world's renewal, then, does not arise from absolute innocence but from a **complex, sometimes contradictory**, inheritance. This challenges simple understandings of who is worthy of salvation. Even in the presence of confusion and shadowy origins, God works through what is broken or misunderstood.

Take the idea that human nature is shaped by ancestry. The presence of wives with ties to the "daughters of men" after the flood might suggest **why post-flood humanity struggles** <u>with the same weakness</u> seen before—envy, violence, ambition, but also the ability to dream and create. Cultural legends across ages echo this mixed legacy. Children of unknown mothers often hold both the burden and the promise of a new chapter. Within the Ark, the unnamed women might have offered perspectives forged in struggle, empathy grown from memories of discord, or wisdom earned in times of chaos.

Consider the mix of legacies inside the Ark. **On one side**, there is <u>Noah, who finds favor in God's eyes</u>. **On the other**, <u>possible echoes of a lineage that once aroused certain concern</u>. The wives, silent and unnamed, bridge these histories, becoming the vessels through which salvation flows. Their influence likely stretches beyond childbearing. Perhaps they steadied their husbands when doubt crept in, recalled stories that shaped the Ark's new rules, or instilled traditions filtering into every nation born after the rain stopped.

This bridging function finds echoes across scripture. Other unnamed or unexpected women change the story's direction—like the servant girl in Naaman's house, or the mother of Samson. Their value lies not in origin or status, but in how they carry hope forward. People shaped by dashed expectations or tangled histories can still become the agents God chooses to use. The lineage of Noah's wives, with its hidden strands, hints that God's pattern is to redeem what the world calls irredeemable.

For readers confronting their own backgrounds—marked by uncertainty, loss, or stigma—the story opens space to see truth and grace working through unlikely channels. The anonymous women become signs that no history is beyond redemption, and that the silence of the past does not erase the importance of those who survive, nurture, and rebuild faith after the storms. Every anonymous figure in the story, then, is an invitation: to wonder what valuable strengths and new beginnings lie hidden in the places where names are missing and histories are incomplete.

Summary & Reflection of this Topic

Now that we have explored the silent presence and profound mystery of **Noah's wife and his daughters-in-law**, we can appreciate how their unnamed roles invite us to look deeper into the story of survival and renewal. **Their anonymity** challenges us to consider the powerful impact of those who work quietly behind the scenes—women whose faithfulness and resilience helped shape humanity's future even **when history forgets their names**. By embracing these unanswered questions, readers are encouraged to see biblical stories not only as ancient records but as living narratives that call us to reflect on themes of grace, redemption, and the hidden strength found in everyday acts of love and courage. This fresh perspective opens new paths for discussion and discovery, helping us recognize that every voice, named or unnamed, holds a vital place in the unfolding story of faith.

Reference List of Chapter 13

Biblical Reference:

Genesis 6:18 *"But I will establish my covenant with you, and you shall come into the ark, you, your sons,* **your wife, and your sons' wives** *with you". – New American Standard* **Bible**

Other References:

Ciobanu, E. (2018, January 1). *Noah's Wife in the Flood Plays: The Body of Argument Between Argumentum ad Verecundiam, Argumentum ad Hominem and Argumentum ad Baculum.* Springer EBooks; Springer Nature.

Tiemeyer, L.-S. (2017, May 12). *Retelling Noah and the Flood: A Fictional Encounter with Genesis 6-9.* Relegere: Studies in Religion and Reception.

The Women of Noah in Early Twentieth-Century Science Fiction – Journal for Interdisciplinary Biblical Studies. (2022, July 19). Hcommons.org.

Chapter 14:

Strange

"Extraordinary Global

Phenomenon"

Genesis 7:4

... *"I will make __the rains__ 'pour down on the earth'. And __it will rain__ for __forty days and forty nights__, until I have wiped from the earth all the living things I have created." –* NLT (Bible)

No Rain Before? Not a Global Diluvian Inundation Before?

Rain for 40 days & 40 nights? That's impossible! Noah's neighbors might have (possibly) said, shaking their heads at the very idea. **Imagine** a world, where water (possibly) didn't fall from the sky in the form of rain, as we experience it today, but rose gently from the earth itself in a form of vapor. **Where fog/mist irrigated** every vegetation's leaf and the ground, nourishing with such humidity every root as well. 'Perhaps the rain itself did exist already (before the day of the flood)', but in a delicate manner and for short moments, enough for drinking consumption, vital necessities, and irrigations. 'But not in a torrential way, for a continual/unstoppable period of time'. For those living before the flood, the thought of heavy rain pounding down, for 40 days and 40 nights **seemed like strange possibility**, far removed from their calm and steady days. Yet, **something was about to change**—something that would disrupt everything people had known about their world and challenge the limits of their faith and understanding. This chapter invites you to step into that moment of surprise and skepticism, to explore how a single **natural phenomenon event** became a symbol of deep spiritual transformation, **raising questions that continue to puzzle readers** and believers alike.

POSSIBILITY OF INTERPRETATION 1:

Preparation for the Catastrophe

A world without rain might sound impossible now, but the ancient biblical story painted just that kind of environment. **Genesis 2:6** describes how, before the flood, the earth was watered by a "*mist that rose up*" "*from the earth,*" suggesting a system so gentle and constant that it left '**no memory or trace of falling water from the sky**'. People lived surrounded by heavy dew and a lushness that came from the ground itself. Plants flourished because each morning, droplets lingered on every leaf and petal, collected on fields, and seeped slowly down to the roots. There were no stormy skies or pounding heavy rains. Daily life depended on rhythms nobody questioned: fields stayed green, the air didn't smell like rain, and the sky remained mostly clear. When children asked where water for the crops came from, parents would (possibly) point to the shimmer on the grass or the mists twisting across the valleys. This gentle cycle of watering signaled to people that nature was mostly dependable, stable, and peaceful.

José E. Espinoza

First <u>Extraordinary Rain</u>? Or Not rain at all before this time?

Scholars have looked at this story and **wondered if it means rain (possibly) didn't exist at all** <u>before the flood</u> or if the narrative simply focuses on a period of gentle growth and unbroken calm. Either way, these biblical details have shaped **deep theological debates** about <u>how God designed the world in its earliest days</u>. Some faith leaders see the (possibly) lack of rain as a symbol of a creation that matched the innocence of its people, free from dramatic disruption and chaos. This mist, in their view, became a sign of how God cared for creation quietly, almost invisibly. Others point out that a world without rain would make God's later judgment through floodwaters all the more shocking—a sudden break with what people had always known and trusted.

Noah's story stands right at this turning point in the biblical narrative. When God warned him of a flood, **the idea of rain falling from the sky in such magnitude,** <u>must have seemed almost absurd to those around him</u>. **And if this was 'a first time phenomenon',** Noah's neighbors could not have imagined <u>rain</u>—water simply did not fall from above. As Noah began building the ark, **his message that rain would both fall and destroy the world** <u>may have sounded so unfamiliar that it became easy for others to dismiss</u>. People might have asked, "How can water come from the sky when we've only ever seen *'vapor'* rise from the ground?" The lack of precedent for such an event laid the groundwork for deep skepticism. **Noah's message** was not just unfamiliar; it **likely felt impossible**, a fantasy outside anyone's experience.

This doubt mirrors how people today resist or dismiss spiritual ideas that seem too different from their lived realities. Faced with a new way of seeing the world or imagining God, many default to disbelief or even ridicule. In Noah's time, the reaction to his warnings formed a sharp line between faith and mockery. The Genesis account and later lessons (with possibilities of interpretations) describe crowds gathering to laugh openly at him, even as he worked day by day. They made jokes about the giant boat in the middle of dry land, they mocked his message, and they returned again and again only to taunt. The mood was (possibly) not just **skeptical—it was caustic**, with people refusing to consider a future shaped by something as alien as rain. In a way, their mocking laughter and resistance, (possibly) made Noah's isolation complete, showing him as a man standing firm while the world doubted around him.

These reactions have a tragic edge, but also a certain comedy. Prophets throughout biblical history faced similar scorn. New ideas almost always meet resistance, especially when they shake the boundaries of what people believe to be possible or safe. In the case of Noah, the skepticism and hostility point to a deeper theme—the struggle to accept that God can disrupt the everyday and introduce something entirely new.

Rain, in this context, <u>became more than just weather</u>. In the biblical narrative, rain stands for both destruction and promise. It brings judgment as water sweeps over the earth, removing what was corrupt, but the story does not end in absolute loss. After the waters recede, the rainbow appears—a sign that God's justice always includes a chance for renewal, a restored world, and hope for the future. **Water (as rain) cleanses and restarts**, <u>echoing other biblical moments</u> where floods, rivers, or the act of washing symbolize <u>new beginnings</u>.

Assuming as 'if never ever had rained before Noah's time; **the sudden appearance of rain** <u>was not just a physical change</u>. It was a marker of spiritual reality that matched a shift in the relationship between God and his creation. As readers think through the idea of mist giving way to downpour, they are invited to picture how profound upheaval—whether in nature or in the heart—can create the conditions for something new. Behind the story of **the strange phenomenon of the flood**, a question waits: <u>what had to shift in the world itself for such rain to fall</u>, and how did that echo a deeper shift in the lives and faith of the people who witnessed it? The stage is set for an exploration of both physical and spiritual transformation.

POSSIBILITY OF INTERPRETATION 2:

Climate Change Before the Flood

A sense of **mystery always surrounds** <u>what came before the first rainfall</u>. Many **wondered whether the very air was different,** when Noah first spoke of water falling from the sky. <u>Some imagined a world that never knew storms or harsh weather</u>, a place where each day simply flowed into the next without interruption. The biblical account gives a brief glimpse: *"springs/streams came up from the earth (in form of vapor or mist) and watered the whole surface of the ground"* (**Genesis 2:6**), <u>but it does not describe rain</u>. This **absence of the phenomenon of rain**, opens the door to all kinds of possibilities of interpretations and theories—about landscapes covered/irrigated in continually and constant mist, and a climate so steady and gentle that people could barely understand Noah's warnings. For many, the sudden appearance of rain meant a complete upending of what was possible.

Theories about the climate of this primeval world come from both religious commentators and modern scientists. One common idea is that the world before the flood enjoyed a sustained, mild climate much like an endless spring, where mist or underground streams kept vegetation lush and green. Obadiah Sforno, a Renaissance thinker, worked out his theory by blending astronomy, theology, and philosophy. He believed that before the flood, the climate was stable due to the sun's then-circular orbit. This steady pattern allowed plants to thrive and meant human lifespans stretched on for centuries. People were accustomed to a constant climate. It also meant there was little sense of danger or unpredictability to challenge or alert its inhabitants. This environment, made the world feel predictable and rejected to accept any climate change never previewed before.

Faith and science both look for a reason <u>why the flood needed to happen</u>. The scriptures describe a period of moral chaos. Violence and selfishness spread across society, unchecked by hardship or limitation. In a stable sunny world, with constant and never changing water springs, people might have imagined themselves immune to the consequences of their own choices. Theologians like Sforno saw a warning here. As 'he interprets' it, God's response to human "lawlessness" was to physically change the earth's climate—to shift the sun's orbit and bring rapid swings between heat and cold, day and night, summer and winter. Such a change would be both punishment and wake-up call, a reshaping of creation to show that actions have consequences even in the natural.

Secular science, too, <u>investigates how ancient climates might have allowed for radical environmental change</u>. **Theories suggest** that a shift in the planet's tilt, a break in a vapor canopy, or large-scale volcanic activity could have transformed the atmosphere, giving rise to sudden rainfall and vast flooding. Fossil records and geological strata hint at periods when ecosystems collapsed rapidly, supporting the possibility of catastrophic change. These ideas help make sense of a flood narrative not just as legend, but as a possible reflection of real environmental upheaval, whether by the impact of strong continuous rain, or breaking of vast natural reservoirs. It becomes a story about a world unprepared for change, where disbelief and skepticism blind people to oncoming disaster.

Noah perhaps did try to persuade a society rooted in comfort and routine that their reality could change. His struggle parallels the challenge of speaking about future risks when there is no precedent. **Faith**, in this sense, is the courage to heed warnings about <u>what has never been seen</u>. The flood story calls readers to reflect on what happens when stability breeds neglect, and when spiritual indifference has practical consequences for both planet and people. These ancient warnings call for humility, vigilance, and ethical responsibility. **Both faith and science** urge people to reconsider their place in creation and the effects of their choices—before the sky opens once more.

Summary & Reflection of this Topic

Now that we have explored the mysterious nature of rain and its **sudden arrival** in the biblical **flood** story, we can better appreciate how this change marks a <u>profound shift in both the natural world</u> and human faith. The mist that once irrigated the earth gave way to a **powerful downpour (rain) of 40 days and 40 nights,** that challenged people's understanding and trust, forcing them to face the <u>reality of judgment and renewal</u>. This chapter invites us to consider how moments of upheaval—whether in nature or spirit—call for courage, reflection, and openness to new truths. As we move forward, let us carry these lessons into our own journeys, embracing the questions and challenges that deepen our connection to the stories of faith, and inspiring thoughtful conversations about the **mysteries that shape our world** and beliefs.

Reference List of Chapter 14

Biblical Reference:

Genesis 7:4 ... ***"I will make <u>the rains</u> pour down on the earth**. And <u>it will rain</u> for forty days and forty nights, until I have wiped from the earth all the living things I have created."* – New Living Translation of **the Bible**

Other References:

After the Flood - Jewish Theological Seminary. (2022, October 26). Jewish Theological Seminary.

Ituma, E. A. (2013). *Christocentric Ecotheology and Climate Change.* Open Journal of Philosophy

Picray, S. (2010, October 25). *Did Noah Warn People About the Flood?* Words of Truth.

The Rainbow as a Token in Genesis | Religious Studies Center. (2018). Byu.edu.

José E. Espinoza

PART 4:

Hour of

The Final Act

Chapter 15:

Strange "Task"

Finalized

Genesis 7:5

"So Noah did everything as The LORD commanded him" – **NLT** *(Bible)*

Obedience Demonstrating Faith

What does it take to accomplish a task so vast and challenging that it demands not only skill but **unwavering faith?** How does someone prepare to face doubt, physical hardship, and the weight of responsibility while following instructions that seem almost impossible to fulfill? These questions invite us to explore how human ability and divine direction come together to achieve something extraordinary. In this chapter, we examine **how one man's talents and trust** in guidance beyond himself enabled him to complete a mission that changed history—showing that **success often lies where preparation meets purpose** and obedience meets hope.

POSSIBILITY OF INTERPRETATION 1:

Noah's Skills and Training

Noah's story unfolds **during an age marked by chaos and darkness**, when <u>corruption, violence, and selfishness reigned across the earth.</u> Out of this world or social environment, Noah stood apart because of qualities passed down and shaped by experience. **He is first known as a builder**. The sheer scale of constructing the ark—an immense structure with space for countless animals—meant <u>Noah could not have started as a novice.</u> In a world without modern machinery, he needed to cut, shape, and join timber using only tools made by hand. Genesis never mentions Noah fumbling through the basics, which hints at generations of practical knowledge running through his family line—likely stretching back to Adam and his early descendants, who lived long lives and passed their skills down.

Noah would have drawn from memories of structures built by great-great-grandparents, perhaps stories of how Enoch or others fashioned homes, storage sheds, and animal pens. Tools probably included axes of stone or bone, sinew cord, clay or metal wedges, and levers crafted from strong branches. To make the planks watertight, bitumen, tar, or tree resin could have been boiled and brushed between seams, a technique found in ancient boat-building. It's not just about knowing how to saw or hammer; a project so vast needed a systematic mind. **Noah had to measure, calculate, and adjust** as the months wore on, planning everything from the size of troughs to the width of walking paths inside the ark for animals of every shape and size. If he neglected any detail, the result could be chaos, wasted materials, or disaster when the rains came.

A keen understanding of nature went hand in hand with Noah's building. Caring for so many living things, **as commanded by God**, called for careful thought and observation. Long before stepping into the ark, Noah had to notice seasonal changes, study animal habits, and prepare ways to manage food and waste for every kind of creature. For example, he could not pack feed randomly; he needed to calculate how much grain, hay, or fresh greens each animal needed for weeks or months. Waste disposal systems had to be organized to prevent sickness and distress. When animals arrived, Noah **probably** observed their moods and grouped them wisely, watched for signs of discomfort, and may have assigned feeding and cleaning tasks to family members with special patience or skill. Gathering and herding diverse animals into the ark would have required trust—a calm presence, still hands, and a voice gentle enough to soothe skittish creatures, while remaining firm in moments of confusion. These practices align with God's vision of stewardship as described in Genesis, where humankind's calling is to care for the world's living inhabitants.

Noah's position as the family's leader was tested by the length and pressure of the ark project. This was not merely a technical assignment; **it was a marathon of patience and courage**. Each family member probably faced private doubts or public scorn. The outside world mocked Noah's work, ridiculed his warnings, and may have threatened his supplies. Keeping his group united required clear communication and the fair assigning of roles. He had to guide, listen, and sometimes resolve hot disagreements. Noah's steady hand set the pace. **He showed up each day**, cloudy day or sunshiny day, hauling tools, making repairs, and setting the same example for young and old alike. By dealing with discouragement and refusing to take shortcuts, Noah won the trust of his sons and their wives. When (possibly) tempers flared or fatigue lingered, he (possibly) turned arguments toward problem-solving, remembered shared commitments, and reminded everyone of the goal. **Through all this**, Noah remained a servant leader—never domineering but always present.

All these abilities emerged from an inner life grounded in faith. Scripture makes it plain that *Noah "walked with God" and lived "blameless" and "righteous" in his generation*. While others (possibly) demanded proof, Noah trusted God's word and set to work. He bore (the possibly mockery), delay, and mystery—working for years with no sign of rain—because he believed a promise greater than his eyes could see. **Noah's routines, discipline, and endurance** were shaped by (possibly constant prayer), reflection, and obedience. This confidence was the bedrock that inspired his family to persist next to him, holding firm against doubts from their neighbors and even from their own tired hearts. Noah's faith guided the small daily choices that made the impossible possible.

Noah's story grows from these practical skills and deep faith, building a bridge between <u>human effort</u> and <u>God's guiding hand</u>. In countless quiet moments—measuring planks, considering all the instructions, encouraging a discouraged son—Noah likely sensed the presence of help beyond himself, drawing out strengths he never thought he had. His preparation and faith became the runway for God's intervention to shape history.

POSSIBILITY OF INTERPRETATION 2:

Divine Guidance in Construction

Noah's story unfolds at the meeting point of preparation and providence, with his capabilities making him ready for a task beyond imagination. As Noah's hands shaped the massive timbers and set the intricate beams, a different dimension was at work—a source of direction and inspiration that reached far past human ingenuity. **The Genesis account starts with God's clear voice**, not just inviting cooperation but providing exact plans for survival. The specifics of these instructions revealed both divine care and the seriousness of the task. Genesis describes God's words: *"Make yourself an ark of cypress wood; make rooms in the ark and coat it with pitch inside and out. This is how you are to build it: The ark is to be three hundred cubits long, fifty cubits wide and thirty cubits high. Make a roof for it, leaving below the roof an opening one cubit high all around. Put a door in the side of the ark and make lower, middle and upper decks."* (**Genesis 6:14-16**).

The list of details could overwhelm anyone. **Carefully prescribed measurements**, material choices, layout—even the number of decks and the use of waterproof pitch—leave nothing to guesswork. – (*Noah* *and the Bible | Noah and the Ark*, n.d.). These instructions were more than technical specifications; they were a sign that God shared the blueprint for hope and deliverance. Noah did not have to invent the method from scratch or wonder about the right approach. God's deep involvement sent a strong message—obedience would lead to safety, and trust in God's way would not come up empty. **The process reveals something profound about their relationship**: Noah's willingness to work closely with **God's details mirrors a deep, personal faith**, one that echoes the earlier description of him as "blameless among his generation." Every cut into the cypress and every stretch of pitch over the planks reaffirmed his faith in a God who gives guidance meant to be followed step by step.

The experience could not have been easy. The ancient world is 'imagined' as noisy with disbelief and mockery. Noah stood apart, watched with skepticism and perhaps even scorn as construction dragged on in the hot sun. The temptation to give up or cut corners must have lurked in the long years of labor. Yet here, divine encouragement makes a difference. Scripture notes that ***"Noah did according to all that God commanded him. So he did."*** (**Genesis 6:22**), a phrase hinting at both obedience and the ongoing willingness to keep going. Trust acts as a sustaining force, and in Noah's solitude, divine comfort may have come in subtle, everyday ways. Maybe a solution to lifting a heavy beam arrived at just the right moment, or maybe he saw renewed determination in his sons' faces when faith wavered. **Spiritual encouragement** becomes as tangible as timber, showing that God's presence offered not only plans but strength to finish the work.

Adversity added pressure from many sides. The task ran up against not just physical limits but emotional ones. **The story invites readers to imagine** the sideways glances, the laughter, and the silent doubts as neighbors passed by the growing structure. How many days did Noah speak to no one but his own family? How many storms, literal or figurative, swept through their camp? The text and tradition both suggest that God's shield extended beyond the structure itself. Divine protection may have taken many forms—a sense of peace replacing fear, wisdom that cut through confusion, or even physical safety from harm. (*Noah and the Bible | Noah and the Ark*, n.d.). With such coverage, Noah kept his balance. He remained able to focus on each day's work without losing sight of the outcome. God's role as protector knit perseverance and hope into the family's daily life, making their resilience more than just human grit.

Beside its practical importance, the ark emerged as a living symbol. Each strike of the hammer was an act of faith, every layer of pitch a visible statement of trust in the unseen. To outsiders, the structure may have looked odd, even foolish before the rain fell. But its shape and permanence announced something powerful: faith means acting on what God has revealed, even when no one else can see the outcome. **The finished ark stood as the meeting place of belief** and material reality—huge, real, and ready when waters came, showing that trust in God brings results built to withstand storms. The story kept growing, reaching back to early figures like Adam and forward to later ones like Moses, whose own basket—the only other "ark" in scripture—offered salvation by water. The ark's legacy now lives not only as a memory of rescue but as a model of what faith looks like when it takes shape in the world, holding space for questions about the ongoing presence of divine involvement in human struggles. (*Noah Moved with Godly Fear*, 2017; *Noah and the Bible | Noah and the Ark*, n.d.).

Summary & Reflection of this Topic

Now that we understand the remarkable blend of Noah's skills, steadfast leadership, and unwavering faith alongside God's precise guidance, we can appreciate how this partnership made a challenging strange task achievable. Noah's story invites us to see that great challenges require both human effort and divine direction working together. As we reflect on his example, we are encouraged to trust in a higher plan even when facing doubt or difficulty, knowing that careful preparation and **faithful obedience** can turn hope into reality. This understanding opens the door for us to explore how lessons from Noah's experience might shape our own journeys of faith and perseverance in times of uncertainty.

Reference List of chapter 15

Biblical Reference:

Genesis 7:5 *"So **Noah did everything** as The Lord Commanded him".* – New Living Translation *of the Bible*

Other References:

Dexter, J. (2022, October 18). *Bible Study on the Life of Noah - Noah Character Study*. Study and Obey.

Lesson, S. S. (2021, April 11). *Monday: The Man Noah – Sabbath School Net*. Ssnet.org.

Noah Moved with Godly Fear. (2017). Churchandfamilylife.com.

Noah And The Bible | Noah And The Ark. (n.d.). The God Who Speaks.

Chapter 16:

Strange "Communication"

(Unknown) (?)

Genesis 7:14–15

*"**They had with them** <u>every wild animal</u> according to its kind, all livestock according to their kinds, **every creature** that moves along the ground according to its kind and every bird according to its kind, everything with wings. Pairs of **all creatures that have the breath of life** in **them** <u>came to Noah</u> and entered the ark"* – **NIV** *(Bible)*

Communication/Connection with *"The Animals" that "came to/with Noah"* to Enter the Ark

As pairs of creatures—beasts, birds, and all manner of living things—approached the massive wooden structure, Noah perhaps did not raise a voice in panic or command. Instead, something far deeper moved through that space: **a connection**, a **communication**, an understanding and comprehension beyond words, drawing each animal forward (to enter the ark) not by force but by some unseen bond. It was as if the chaos of the world had paused, replaced by **a sharp clarity where man and beast met on equal ground**, **communicating** in 'a language' older than time itself. This moment, recorded briefly yet powerfully in ancient scripture, invites us to reconsider what might have been **possible** when creation existed in harmony—where trust, purpose, and comprehension wove creatures and humans into one unified story.

POSSIBILITY OF INTERPRETATION 1:

Noah's Communication with Creatures

Noah stood as the boundary between the old world and the new, entrusted with a calling that few could fathom. **Genesis 7:14–15** tells how *"every beast after its kind, all cattle after their kind, every creeping thing that creepeth upon the earth after his kind, and every fowl after his kind, every bird of every sort. And they went in unto Noah into the ark, two and two of all flesh."* While the text sets the stage, it silently begs the question of how, in the midst of chaos, such astonishing order emerged. Exploring the **mystery** starts with the possibility that Noah's ability to gather and direct the animals stemmed from more than ordinary leadership or practical skill.

If God empowered Noah with a divine gift of communication, the event would exceed the bounds of any everyday experience. The Book of Genesis speaks repeatedly of God's direct instruction to Noah—commands stated with clarity, such as **Genesis 7:1**: *"And the LORD said unto Noah, Come thou and all thy house into the ark."* **Imagine if**, along with these words, came an ongoing spiritual presence allowing Noah to reach the animal world at God's own bidding. The world around Noah might have shifted into sharper focus, where every bleat, low, or wingbeat fit into a silent orchestra of understanding that no human before or since would fully grasp. He might have felt the weight of his chosen role with even greater strength, realizing that his words and gestures, charged with divine import, created a bond recognized by each animal as they approached him. **The animals, too**, may have received their own moment of clarity, moving not in fear or confusion, but as participants of God's design. **Responsibility**, in such a setting, transformed into a living connection between the steward and the creatures—each movement purposeful, each call met with a willing answer, as if Noah and his living charges understood each other's hearts.

Scripture often paints an image of lost unity in creation after the Fall. Before that, humanity and animals lived together without hostility or confusion. Some believe **there may once have been a 'universal language',** a way of speaking that crossed from human to beast and back again. Within this idea, Noah's world belonged to the older order, or at least echoed it by special grace. **Gathering the animals** would involve words, sounds, or expressions that held plain meaning for every creature. The lion would pause, look at Noah, and understand his summons not as a threat but as invitation. **Birds** would hear a tone that brought comfort and certainty, circling down to rest on the Ark's beams. Scenes played out where the animals approached in calm, eyes fixed on the man standing by God's command, and listened for simple instructions: wait here, walk there, enter now. The air brimmed with mutual understanding, as if the distance between every living kind had narrowed for just one moment in time.

Yet even **if spoken language failed**, <u>another kind of direction became possible</u> through instinct guided from above. Genesis hints that *"they went in unto Noah"* not by force or trick, but as if compelled. Animals—guided since birth by inner senses—can flee storms, avoid danger, and navigate long distances with unerring accuracy. Multiply these traits by the will of the Creator, and instinct becomes the bridge across every gap. The creatures might have sensed the change in air, the coming flood, or even the unique presence of Noah himself, drawing them forward without fear or hesitation. Their usual wariness melted before a greater urge, blending natural wisdom with something new. Real world examples give glimpses: birds departing before hurricanes, dogs alerting their owners to storms, or herds moving together in sudden harmony. **In Noah's time**, such instincts grew into something keener, a kind of wisdom that responded to the movements of the divine and the man chosen to lead.

Communication often travels without words, woven through posture, presence, and action. Noah's hands and arms, open in welcome, or his stride toward the Ark might have spoken volumes to the animal mind. Nonverbal cues—a gentle beckon, a stillness, a guiding arm—could become the common tongue. Animals, watchful and sensitive, picked up these signals with almost uncanny precision. Within the Ark's shadow, every gesture took on meaning. One step forward meant approach; a calm stand at the doorway gave permission. Sometimes, symbolic action replaced speech: Noah carrying food, laying straw, or leading a lamb up the ramp might tell the others, "This path is safe." In the midst of this, trust grew on both sides, built from more than habit: it arose from the sacred drama unfolding in that place and time.

All these glimpses point <u>to deeper intellect and awareness in the animal world</u> than many suppose. Something in this ancient scene hints at a world where **communication**, **understanding**, and **purpose** <u>crossed natural boundaries</u>. Readers are left with the sense that the Ark's story calls for a new consideration of creation's hidden depths, with mysteries waiting to be explored further.

POSSIBILITY OF INTERPRETATION 2:

Intellectual Capacity of Pre-Fall Animals

The unusual cooperation between Noah and the animals hints at an ancient world with different expectations for what creatures could understand or do. **If the animals truly recognized God's instructions** and <u>followed Noah's lead</u>, something about their minds must have worked in ways difficult to imagine today. Many people picture animals as driven mainly by instincts—reacting to immediate needs, rarely planning ahead. Yet, **Genesis 7:14-15** and the story of the Ark imply animals responded thoughtfully, organizing themselves and entering quietly, as if they understood the moment's importance. This starts to suggest that in the original creation, animals may have shared in **an intelligence** that allowed for attentive, deliberate choices.

Scripture doesn't give many details, but certain stories nudge the imagination. The serpent in Eden carries out a deceptive **conversation**, (**Genesis 3:2-5.**) <u>showing understanding of cause and effect</u> and enough cunning to influence human actions. While later tradition often links this to spiritual evil, it still paints a picture of a **creature thinking and communicating** far beyond simple reflexes.

In Genesis 6 and 7, when the animals approach Noah, the orderly procession and their willingness to enter the Ark without chaos stand as another sign. Such behavior implies the **ability to grasp new situations**, notice patterns, or recognize Noah as a leader—capacities that go beyond what today's animals demonstrate in the wild. Cognitive abilities like these would have enabled the animals to follow complex requests, trust new routines, and **possibly** even sense the world's coming change.

Moral Understanding and Obedience

Part of what makes the story so striking is the **absence of disorder**. The Ark's filling (at the entering moment) doesn't sound like a frightened stampede; instead, it reads like a trustworthy response to invitation. One theory some scholars and Bible teachers discuss is that pre-Fall animals held a basic sense of right and wrong—not abstract morality as in humans, but a created order that "felt" obedience to God. Where modern animals might only yield to habit or training, those before the Fall may have innately leaned toward what pleased their Maker.

Imagine a line of elephants halting respectfully instead of crowding the entrance, or those we know today as predatory animals protecting and guiding weaker ones nearby. Even the rapid gathering at Noah's call hints that they obey a shared internal cue, similar to how flocks migrate or bees swarm together, but guided here by something deeper—a memory of Eden's order. This idea gives new depth to the Ark narrative. Following Noah wasn't just about fear or food, but a sense of duty or willing participation in a purpose connected to God's larger plan. Such moral awareness would explain how animal chaos never took over, and why harmony could rule even among creatures usually at odds.

Relationships with Humans

The world before the Fall sounds like it ran on relationships—between God and humans, between people, and perhaps between humans and animals too. If creatures then didn't just tolerate humans but felt deep trust or even affection, their response to Noah changes from reluctant compliance to genuine loyalty. Scripture calls **Adam the one who names the animals**, (According to **Genesis 2:19-20**) which many understand as a sign of authority and also **connection.** Imagine if that bond meant the animals felt drawn to help, eager to stay close to people who cared for them and shared their space.

Today, people witness glimpses of this in loyal dogs, working animals, or wild creatures showing curiosity toward kind humans. Multiply that sense by an entire creation and it's easier to picture lions resting at Noah's feet or doves circling him before landing. When stress hit—loud storms, strange crowds, unfamiliar enclosures—these animals might have found calm in their trust of Noah, responding not out of fear but out of relationship.

Adaptability to Communication

The Bible's telling suggests that communication spanned obstacles. God's prompting, Noah's voice, or subtle cues all seemed to matter. A crow might catch a hand signal or a horse heed a spoken word. This adaptability could reflect the world's design to thrive on understanding—a design fragmented after the Fall, but seen fully in moments like Noah's gathering. Some creatures now respond only to single cues or basic routines, but the animals of Genesis responded as if reading the situation, picking up from others, and staying attuned to higher direction.

Examples in nature, even now, show dolphins learning signs, birds copying tunes, and elephants remembering years-old commands. If the first animals were even more receptive—listening to God, pausing at Noah's instruction, adjusting based on the group—it fits a vision of creation meant for harmony. All of these traits together create a picture of a world where Noah's task wasn't just possible, but a real demonstration of the world's original unity, intelligence, and purpose.

Summary & Reflection of this Topic

Now that we have explored the **remarkable communication** between <u>Noah and the animals</u>, we can begin to see a world where harmony between humans and creatures was not only possible but deeply rooted in God's original design. **This understanding** invites us to consider the <u>ancient bond that bridged species</u> through purpose, trust, and obedience—a bond that calls us to rethink how creation once worked together in unity. As we reflect on this **extraordinary moment before the flood**, we are challenged to look beyond the familiar and open ourselves to the **mysteries** of faith and creation, encouraging deeper study and fresh conversations about the powerful relationship between humanity, the animal world, and the divine plan unfolding in Genesis.

José E. Espinoza

References of Chapter 16

Biblical References:

Genesis 7:14–15

"They had with them <u>every wild animal</u> according to its kind, all livestock according to their kinds, **every creature** that moves along the ground according to its kind and every bird according to its kind, everything with wings. 15 Pairs of **all creatures that have the breath of life** in **them** <u>came to Noah</u> and entered the ark" – New International Version of <u>the Bible</u>

Genesis 2:19-20

"And out of the ground **the LORD God** formed <u>every beast of the field, and every fowl of the air;</u> and **brought them unto Adam** <u>to see what he would call them</u>: <u>and whatsoever Adam called every living creature</u>, **that was the name thereof**. 20 And **Adam gave names** <u>to all cattle, and to the fowl of the air, and to every beast of the field</u>; ... " – KJV (Bible)

Genesis 3:2-5

"And **the woman said unto the serpent**, We may eat of the fruit of the trees of the garden: 3 But of the fruit of the tree which is in the midst of the garden, God hath said, Ye shall not eat of it, neither shall ye touch it, lest ye die. 4 And **'the serpent said' unto the woman**, Ye shall not surely die":... – KJV (Bible)

Chapter 17:

Strange

"Closing of the Door"

<u>Genesis 7:16</u>

... *"<u>The LORD God Closed the Door</u>".* – NLT (Bible)

What Hand or What Force Did Close the Door?

Have you ever paused to wonder about the moment the **Ark's door was shut**, <u>not by human hands</u> but (possibly) **by <u>the hand of God Himself?</u>** What might it mean for Noah and his family that they could no longer open or close this door once it was sealed? **Why does this act carry such weight** in the story of the flood, beyond just a simple barrier against water? Could there be deeper lessons about **trust, protection, and finality** hidden behind that closing moment? These questions invite us to look beyond the surface and explore the **significance of God's deliberate action**—a divine boundary between judgment and mercy, between the world that was and the new beginning promised inside the Ark. As we consider this moment together, we will uncover how **this closed door** <u>marks a turning point</u> where faith meets fate, and how it continues to challenge us to recognize God's authority and steadfast care in times of uncertainty.

POSSIBILITY OF INTERPRETATION 1:

<u>Significance</u> of <u>God's Action</u> in Genesis 7:16

A handwritten command sealed away the world as Noah knew it. **The moment God closed the Ark's door**, the story of old <u>earth reached its most decisive turning point</u>. When Noah and his household entered the Ark, <u>God's action drew a clear line</u>. No human hands shut them in, **signaling that what came next was out of human reach or choice**. The moment <u>God took control of the door</u>, a display of **authority and power** unfolded—something only He could do. This decision separated Noah's trust-filled obedience from the outside world's disbelief, placing everyone's fate wholly in His grasp.

Looking at the literal door, wooden and massive, creaking on its hinges, **it meant more than simple protection** from rising waters. <u>Its closing was a statement—God alone determines the moment chances end</u>. All announcements, all warnings, and all invitations up to this point pointed at a coming choice. But in that instant, with the groan of ancient timbers and a lock tightened by unseen hands, there was no more deciding, pleading, or bargaining. **This was a final verdict**. For the world outside, the closed door marked the last ignored plea for mercy. <u>Grace transformed into irreversible judgment,</u>

and the opportunity for **new beginnings** narrowed, now resting with the eight human beings inside de arc.

Inside the Ark, a sense of safety replaced the tension of waiting. Yet even in this safety, there may have been silent prayers—questions about loved ones left outside, or about what the future would look like once the deluge ended. Noah and his family poassibly faced deep uncertainty. Still, the hand that closed the door represented loving purpose, not only judgment. God's personal intervention told Noah, and everyone who would read the story in times to come, that rescue and assurance come by divine promise, not by accident or luck.

At this moment, Noah and his family became recipients of God's deep faithfulness. **Even in the face of world-changing destruction**, <u>God shielded those who followed Him</u>. This assurance, handmade in history, echoed promises that would repeat again—Abraham's descendants shielded in Egypt, Daniel protected in Babylon, a remnant saved through coming trials. God closing the Ark's door pointed forward toward other covenants, where preservation and new life would rise from chaos.

Noah found this safety not by his strength, but <u>because **God remembered him**</u> and fulfilled His word. The outside world, in contrast, experienced a point of no return. When the rain started, the physical barrier drove home the reality of each one's choices. People who had watched the Ark's construction, 'maybe' mocking or shrugging it off, realized the door was sealed—not by a neighbor or chief, but by God Himself. **The authority belonged to God alone**.

<u>This was, in one sense, the ultimate divine boundary</u>: the door neither Noah nor others could open or close after the decision arrived.

For early readers of Genesis and for those hearing it now, the closing door stands as a symbol of time-limited grace. It brings a sobering reminder: <u>second chances are rich valuable gifts</u>, not endless cheap supplies. Reflecting on the moment when the Ark's door closed, there is a personal challenge. Every life has seasons when the opportunity to respond, to turn, or to seek shelter in God's promises moves out of reach. **Those inside were called (after) righteous by faith (Hebrews 11:7),** <u>having trusted and prepared</u> despite not seeing what was ahead. Those outside had ignored seasons of warning, believing there would be more time.

The echo of the **closed door** can resonate during moments of crisis or transition. In the Ark, eight people waited out the storm, shielded from judgment by a <u>shelter built in faith</u> and sealed in hope. Their experience reminds readers that, even when fear and uncertainty swirl outside, God's protection is sure. Even as creation trembled, the family inside the Ark lived within the circle of God's promise. In troubled times, the same reassurance stands ready—the faithfulness that preserved Noah reaches across ages, offering a new path forward to anyone willing to step inside and trust the door closed by God's hand alone. Each step into such grace offers a shelter, and every moment of protection flows from God's deliberate, loving authority, inviting people to recognize the power and wonder of true divine assurance.

POSSIBILITY OF INTERPRETATION 2:

Protection for Those Inside

The moment **God closes the door of the Ark** in **Genesis 7:16** carries a sense of <u>finality</u>, but the deeper story is what takes place after the latch is shut. Inside, Noah, his wife, his sons, and daughters-in-law become witnesses to a world dividing into two—the outside condemned to chaos, the inside held by promise and protection. **The Ark**, <u>sealed by God's own action</u>, serves as an unmistakable boundary **separating judgment from mercy**, loss from life, and despair from security. Left behind are the storm and clamor of a world that refused to listen; within the Ark's walls, God prepares a place where human and animal life are set apart so they might continue.

Raindrops and floodwaters hammer against the exterior of the Ark, carrying debris, the cries of the storm, and all the weight of the old world's end, but nothing breaches the shelter crafted by divine command. **The very act of shutting the door** is a gesture of <u>absolute protection</u>. When the waters rise and the land vanishes, the Ark does not falter; inside, order replaces the destruction that swirls outside. The family and their animal companions experience a pause they can trust. They are free to tend to the daily needs of life—feeding, cleaning, nurturing—without fear of being swept away, for God's hand secures their safety at the most physical, elemental level. Picture the contrast between the violent surge outside and the steady, watchful care within, where each meal and each moment of sleep reflects the reality of God's shelter.

Beyond safety from physical disaster, the Ark acts as a spiritual cocoon. The world outside was not only troubled by the waters, but by corruption, violence, and estrangement from God. Here, in the vessel of salvation, **God's grace becomes not only a shield, but a daily presence**. The family learns what it means to be set apart, marked as recipients of mercy rather than judgment. The Ark transforms from a mere construction project into a sacred sanctuary. Every echo of floodwaters becomes a reminder that they did not find themselves on the Ark by accident—they were **chosen**, favored, and **preserved**. In this space, separated from all that defiled the earth, they encounter grace not as an abstract idea, but as lived experience, much like how the Temple would later be a place to sense God's nearness or how refuge cities provided sanctuary during crises. The Ark is the only place in the world untouched by the chaos outside, marking it as a holy site of hope.

God's closing of the Ark's door is a visible pledge to keep His covenant. Before the flood ever came, God declared that this rescue would be part of a larger story—a line of faithfulness connecting generations. **Sealing the Ark** is not just about keeping Noah's family dry and alive; it's about securing the thread of promise that will run from Noah down to Abraham to Israel and, much later, to all who would call upon God through Jesus Christ. **By acting, God draws a line around His chosen**, <u>preserving them in order to fulfill every word He has spoken about rescue, renewal, and future blessing</u>. The Ark becomes a living sign of the ongoing story of salvation found in other moments of biblical history—a precursor to the basket that saved Moses on the Nile, and even the image of Christ as the vessel who saves from judgment. Each time, divine initiative ensures the promise remains unbroken, not because of human achievement, but because God acts and protects.

All the while, the door remains closed by God's choice, not their own. This one action gives Noah's family the gift of knowing their rescue is not their own doing, but God's. Inside, they rest in the knowledge that while the world outside churns with uncertainty, they remain held within a promise, protected for a reason far greater than mere survival.

Summary & Reflection of this Topic

Now that we understand the profound meaning behind **God closing the Ark's door**, we can see how this moment marks both <u>an ending and a new beginning</u>—where divine authority sets the course and the idea for salvation and judgment alike. This act teaches us that protection and promise come not from human effort but from trusting in God's faithful hand, even when the future is uncertain. As we reflect on Noah's story, we are invited to recognize the times in our own lives when doors close and grace moves from invitation to assurance, challenging us to respond with faith and readiness. Embracing this understanding encourages us to find hope and purpose amid life's storms, **knowing that just as God preserved Noah and his family**, <u>He offers ongoing protection and renewal</u> for all who step within the shelter of His promises.

Reference List of Chapter 17

Biblical Reference:

Genesis 7:16

*... **"Then the LORD closed the door behind them"**. - New Living Translation **(of the Bible)***

Other references:

Bradshaw, J. M. (2021, March 29). *The Ark and the Tent: Temple Symbolism in the Story of Noah | The Interpreter Foundation.*

Genesis 7 Commentary | Precept Austin. (2024). Preceptaustin.org.

Jonas Sello Thinane. (2023, October 20). *Noah's Ark to the Great Commission: Defusing Xenophobia in South Africa.* Journal of Religious and Theological Studies/E-Journal of Religious and Theological Studies.

Playing Noah | Animal Legal & Historical Center. (2025). Animallaw.info.

Chapter 18:

Strange

'Extermination/Renovation'

Genesis 7:23-24.

*"**God wiped out (Exterminated)** every living thing on the earth—people, livestock, small animals that scurry along the ground, and the birds of the sky. **All were destroyed**. The only people who survived were Noah and those with him in the boat. (24) And the floodwaters covered the earth for 150 days" – **NLT** (Bible)*

Before The Flood; Genesis 5-7

A Reality of Inevitability

"He blotted out (Exterminated) every living thing that was on the face of the ground." These words from **Genesis 7:23** echo with a sense of **finality** and silence, <u>painting a picture of a world suddenly emptied except for one family and a handful of animals</u>. The story of the Flood is familiar to many, but these closing verses leave us with more questions than answers. What does it mean when **everything is wiped away**? How can survival exist alongside total destruction? And what hope can emerge from such a **strange ending**?

This chapter invites readers to explore these difficult questions by looking closely at <u>the meaning behind the biblical Flood's conclusion</u>. It considers different ways people have understood this moment—from seeing it as a symbol of judgment, to recognizing the importance of a faithful remnant, to appreciating the tension in its uncertain and open-ended nature. By examining **Genesis 7:23-24** carefully, young adults and Bible study groups are encouraged to think deeply about how this ancient story still speaks to themes of loss, hope, and **new beginnings** today.

Exploring Interpretations of the Biblical Flood

Genesis 7:23-24 reads: *"He blotted out (Exterminated) every living thing that was on the face of the ground, man and animals and creeping things and birds of the heavens. They were blotted out from the earth. Only Noah was left, and those who were with him in the ark. And the waters prevailed on the earth 150 days."* These verses stand at the closing of **the Flood story's great crescendo**, leaving behind an image of utter erasure—of life, beauty, and potential, all swept away **(Exterminated)** except for one preserved remnant. <u>The language is arresting in how absolute it feels</u>, pushing readers to wonder if this is the end of a story or the **strange beginning of something new**. The text's finality, and its sudden silence about all save Noah, have fueled centuries of questions: **Why such drastic action?** How does survival work against obliteration? Does the ending point to despair, grace, or both at once?

José E. Espinoza

POSSIBILITY OF INTERPRETATION 1:

Total Disapproval by the Creator and Owner of The Planet & Humanity

<u>One way</u> readers have interpreted these verses is as a statement of total judgment—a divine act of cleansing that leaves nothing behind **except what God chooses to spare**. *"He blotted out every living thing..."* echoes, in its starkness, other moments in the Hebrew Bible where God's judgment is described as all-encompassing. *For example, the destruction of *Sodom and Gomorrah in **Genesis 19:25** similarly wipes out tow entire cities, with only Lot and his family surviving due to divine intervention. In Exodus, the *final plague claims every Egyptian firstborn but spares those protected by God's command (Exodus 12:29-30). (*Topics that will be explored later; in sub-sequential books related to this serie) Taking this approach, **Genesis 7:23-24** signals that when evil or corruption reaches a certain point, <u>the only solution</u> is a **radical restart**—the world must be re-set for goodness and justice to have a chance. This view often frames <u>God's action here as motivated by profound sorrow (pain)</u> but also strict fairness: **Genesis 6:5** describes the earth being *"filled with violence,"* necessitating dramatic intervention. Some theologians underline that while judgment seems harsh, <u>mercy shines through the</u>

provision of the ark, which becomes an emblem of hope and possible salvation for those who respond to God's invitation (see also Hebrews 11:7, linking Noah's faith to the possibility of rescue). In Bible study groups, young adults might compare this to the idea of having to "wipe and restore" a corrupted device: sometimes, everything malfunctions so completely that only a hard reset can save what's valuable and accomplish the designated purpose.

José E. Espinoza

POSSIBILITY OF INTERPRETATION 2:

The Plan: (Kingdom of God on Earth) Continue with a New Remnant

A second interpretation highlights the theme of faithful remnant rather than only focusing on destruction. This reading points out that *"Only Noah was left, and those who were with him in the ark,"* drawing attention to God's pattern throughout scripture of preserving a faithful group even in the bleakest circumstances. In **Isaiah 10:20-22**, the prophet speaks of a remnant returning after judgment, suggesting that even in loss, <u>God's purpose moves forward through a chosen few</u>. The survival of Noah's family shifts the focus from the scale of the flood's destruction to the hope that sprouts in the aftermath. **Romans 11:5-6** uses similar language, describing those who remain faithful not through their own strength but through grace. Here, **the Flood's ending is not just about erasing wickedness**; <u>it is about God's ongoing commitment</u>, carried by regular people who trust enough to follow instructions, even when they are strange or risky. This way of reading might prompt young adults to consider how in times of "flood"—whether personal crisis, community upheaval, or periods of doubt—sticking close to God and staying together as a group preserves something precious that can grow again.

The ark, in this sense, becomes not only a lifeboat but a community project, much like the way a group project at school or work can feel both <u>risky and protective</u> when the world outside seems chaotic.

Understanding Rarity and Strangeness

A story that ends not with a slow return to normal, but with the sweeping erasure of almost all (previous) life leaves a mark in a way few ancient tales attempt. **Genesis 7:23-24** presents such a moment— everything outside of one family and a handful of creatures is wiped out, and the world sits silent under water for a full 150 days. This event pushes far beyond the boundaries of ordinary disaster stories known in the ancient world. Floods, fires and wars often fill early literature, but the scale of Genesis stands in a league of its own, both in <u>detail and in intention</u>.

The Hebrew telling highlights the deliberate preservation of Noah and his household, set against the vastness of all else being erased. Rather than portraying a cycle of violence or chaos, as many other stories do, **Genesis places a reset** at the center—an intentional stopping and restarting, as if the entire world is a stage swept blank for a new act.

The Bible takes care to underline the math of destruction. *"Every living thing that moved on land perished– birds, livestock, wild animals, all the creatures that swarm over the earth, and all mankind"* (**Genesis 7:21**). By stating the sum and listing the kinds, the writer paints a picture of all corners of the landscape, all types and categories, engulfed. The one exception, Noah and those with him, highlights the contrast so sharply that readers can hardly miss its point. This stands out against ancient disaster epics' usual chaos, where survivors either trickle by accident or fate, and the gods' actions often feel less clear in moral purpose.

POSSIBILITY OF INTERPRETATION 3:

Besides 40 Days Rain, 150 Days Inundation

Adding to this rarity is <u>the detail about time</u>. The flood does not subside in a few days or weeks; it lingers for 150 days, (5 Month approximately in our days' time measure) a detail repeated to stress both duration and discomfort. The survivors cannot simply wade out when the rain ends, nor can they know the future as the waters continue. This extended interval of waiting puts Noah and his family in an unfamiliar place—hanging between eras, not knowing what the world will look like after. Many ancient tales mention quick recoveries after wrath or calamity, but here, hope is stretched to its longest length, testing human patience and trust.

In this account, the notion of "<u>all living things</u>" underlines the breadth of the tragedy. This is not just about the loss of a city, as with Sodom and Gomorrah, nor a tribe, nor even a kingdom. Every animal, bird, and human outside the vessel perishes, and the **planet itself changes face and Climate**. Such a sweep would break the mental boundaries of those hearing it in ancient times—few could have imagined a world in which only one boat of survivors floats above total silence. The loss described would stun listeners, calling them to think not only of mortality, but also of what makes a life worth preserving.

Yet, in this strangeness, <u>Genesis invites questions that linger long after details fade</u>. What does it mean for God to choose to save a single household while everything else ends? Is survival a reward, a trust, or a burden? By isolating Noah and his family, the narrative opens a space for readers to consider both individual and communal roles in the unfolding story of faith.

This moment, <u>where the world pauses</u> **for 150 days**, also echoes with larger biblical themes. Later in Genesis, in the aftermath of Babel or with the calling of Abraham, God's involvement remains personal, but never again does the earth itself serve as a canvas for such a total rewrite. The flood, then, becomes a singular event—the hinge between what was and what may still be possible. It brings to mind Lamentations' questions about destruction and hope, or the prophets' promises of restoration after exile. **Even Jesus will later refer to Noah's days** <u>to make sense out of coming upheaval</u>, using this story's weight to talk about readiness, justice, and new beginnings.

Experiencing the record of this flood (global Inundation), readers are pressed to face both the limits of human understanding and the reach of divine mystery. The text does not shrink from describing the cost, nor does it offer easy comfort. Instead, it honors the sorrow and fear of loss while lifting up the hope of survival, **the promise of another chance** growing even while the waters remain high. In this waiting, the story becomes an invitation—can new beginnings rise after the most impossible endings, and what does such a story say about the One who holds both justice and mercy together?

In classrooms and study groups, this ending challenges every generation to take its questions further. The flood in Genesis is no ordinary story, not in its time nor ours. **It is the strangeness of a world reset** and a call to consider what it would feel like to float in that long, anxious waiting, uncertain but carried onward by a promise greater than any storm.

José E. Espinoza

Summary & Reflection of this Topic

Now that we have explored the rich and complex meanings behind **Genesis 7:23-24**, we can approach this powerful story not only as an ancient account of destruction but as **a living invitation to reflect on judgment, hope, and renewal**. Understanding the flood's total impact alongside the survival of Noah's faithful remnant, helps us see how this narrative <u>challenges us to trust in new beginnings</u> even when circumstances seem overwhelming. For young adults and study groups alike, this passage opens space to ask difficult questions about faith, justice, and mercy, encouraging us to hold uncertainty with patience while awaiting what comes next. By engaging deeply with these themes, we prepare ourselves to carry the lessons of the flood into our own lives and communities, ready <u>to face the unknown</u> with both **courage and hope**.

Reference List of Chapter 18

Biblical Reference:

Genesis 7:23-24.

*"**God wiped out** every living thing on the earth—people, livestock, small animals that scurry along the ground, and the birds of the sky. **All were destroyed**. The only people who survived were Noah and those with him in the boat. 24 And the floodwaters covered the earth for 150 days" – New **L**iving **T**ranslation of the Bible*

Other References:

Escolà-Gascón, Á. (2020, November). *Researching unexplained phenomena II: new evidences for anomalous experiences supported by the Multivariable Multiaxial Suggestibility Inventory-2 (MMSI-2)*. Current Research in Behavioral Sciences.

Gillard, D. (2017). *Deconstructing the Bible: interpretive possibilities*. Education-Uk.org.

Heatley, K. (2023, February 27). *MIT physicists predict exotic new phenomena and give "recipe" for realizing them*. MIT Physics.

Conclusion

Throughout history, some stories have outlasted empires. The flood narrative and the **strange topics** woven throughout **Genesis 5–7** are such stories—echoes from a world that now feels impossibly distant, yet teeming with puzzles that continue to spark curiosity and debate. **To close our journey through these ancient enigmas**, let us pause not merely to summarize what we've explored, but to gather the threads into something lasting: a renewed invitation to wonder, to question, and to live with deeper awareness.

At every stage of this book, **strangeness has been our guide**. We met descendants whose names were never given to be known, shadows in the scriptural record who nonetheless shaped human history. Their lives, hinted at only briefly, challenge us to look for meaning beyond the obvious and to recognize that, even in silence operations, people matter. The invisible contributions of **Adam's unnamed sons and daughters** remind us that history is made as much by those in the background as those at center stage, and that every community stands on the quiet work of many unseen hands.

We encountered Enoch—a figure who vanished, his fate cloaked **in mystery**. His story forced us to ask what it means to <u>walk with God</u>, to live faithfully amid confusion, and to imagine a future shaped not by certainty but commitment. **Enoch's disappearance** troubles the boundary between earthly mortality and hope for more, suggesting that life with God can open doors into the unknown, where faith becomes a journey shaped as much by questions as answers.

Then, just before the flood changed everything, we delved into tangled identities and relationships: the **daughters of men**, the **enigmatic sons of God**, and a generation marked by the dilemma of beauty, ambition, and blurred boundaries.

The flood itself stands as the great dividing line—a **response to corruption** so total that only radical transformation could offer hope. Yet, even here, Genesis refuses to settle for easy villain and hero narratives. Instead, it presses us to consider divine patience: **the offer of 120 years**, the persistent calls to repentance, and the struggle to live wisely within numbered days. Here, time takes on a sacred urgency, reminding us that each season is not endless, and that opportunities for change carry both risk and promise.

Amid warnings and judgment, we find a stubborn hope: God chooses a remnant, <u>one family led by **a man character and justice; Noah**</u>. Imagine the strangeness of this—the whole world narrowed to a handful of believers, a few pairs of animals, and a boat afloat in chaos. Noah's justice was not flashy or dramatic; rather, he modeled daily faithfulness, grounded in routine obedience, even when others possibly despised such conduct. It's a portrait of integrity not isolated from community but deepened by the tension of standing apart. In highlighting **Noah's solitude or singularity**, Genesis nudges readers to reflect: What does it mean to do right when nobody else will? How might we, in our own small corners, step forward as bearers of hope and renewal?

The details of the Ark—its **mysterious (unidentified) wood**, vast size, and meticulous construction—invoke wonder about lost knowledge and forgotten worlds. **Gopher wood**, <u>mentioned only once</u> in all of scripture, opens a window onto ancient forests, extinct species, and the theme of stewardship that winds through every page. The Ark's assembly brings together human skill and divine guidance, a lesson in trusting instructions whose reasons may remain hidden until much later. Through Noah, we see that transformative action often requires attention to detail, resilience in the face of mockery, and a willingness to build toward an end no one else expects.

But the flood narrative is not only a story of beginnings and endings. It also whispers about communication that transcends boundaries—between humans and animals, between those inside and outside, between the present and the futures yet to come. **As the animals entered the Ark**, we glimpsed <u>the possibility of a world bound by trust and mutual understanding</u>, echoing the harmony first imagined in Eden. These moments encourage us to seek reconciliation not only with each other but with all creation, attentive to the ways we are linked in the story God continues to tell.

We cannot ignore, either, the weight of endings that feel absolute. **The Ark's door shut by God himself** marks a point of final decision—where grace yields to judgment, and the chance to choose gives way to the consequences of earlier choices. Genesis paints this not with glee but **regret,** showing us a Creator grieved over brokenness, yet refusing to leave chaos unchallenged. **"He blotted out (exterminated) every living thing,"** says the text—devastation on a scale that silences even the bravest interpreters. And still, after the torrent ceases, the world waits—silent, empty, and uncertain. Out of this void, the seeds for new life and new relationship are planted, patiently nurtured in a vessel that floated above destruction.

For the young adults, study groups, and seekers of mystery who have taken this journey, these episodes offer more than facts to memorize. They provide, instead, a set of mirrors and windows: mirrors revealing the ongoing struggles with pride, compromise, loneliness, and hope that mark every generation; windows opening out onto the depth and dimension of **a God who both judges and rescues**, who regrets but also renews. These stories ask us to be honest about our own times—the pressures that draw us away from what is right, the subtle costs of pursuing power or surface beauty, the challenges of holding to integrity when certainty and justice fails.

Yet perhaps **the greatest gift of Genesis' strange topics** is their refusal to give neat or definitive answers. **Mystery lingers at every turn**. The unknown descendants, enigmatic heroes, silent wives, and extraordinary natural events summon us not to solve every puzzle once and for all, but to keep returning—to wrestle, to discuss, to imagine, and even to pray. Through ambiguity and wonder, we are drawn closer to the heart of faith, where asking matters as much as resolving, and where stories teach us not only what happened, but how to stay curious and receptive.

As you share these chapters in your study groups or ponder them individually by your own, remember: the questions that trouble you most are often the doors to deeper wisdom. **The stories of Genesis** endure not because they answer everything, but because they open space for fresh encounters—with scripture, with the world, and with the One whose presence fills even the <u>strangest mysteries with purpose</u>.

May you walk away from this book with bolder faith, a greater appetite for seeking truth, and renewed readiness to honor both the seen and the hidden—the named and the nameless, the clear and the uncertain—in the grand and unfolding drama of God's story. (this is the greatest desire of the author of this book; Jose E. Espinoza). For in exploring the peculiar, we discover again that **the greatest mysteries are not roadblocks**, <u>but invitations to encounter grace</u>, justice, and the surprising newness always waiting on the far side of the storm.

About The Author

José E. Espinoza is a Writer, Instructor, and Christian guide specializing in **Leadership** and personal development for young believers, experienced individuals, and professionals in the walk of faith. He has been a dedicated **Missionary** since his youth, consistently committed to sharing **the Evangelical Message of The Kingdom of God.**

José E. Espinoza

Other books from The Author

Available on Amazon:

RARE CASES Book #1

In the New Testament with Possibilities of Interpretations; on Passages of Intrigue and Enigma in the 4 Gospels

STRANGE TOPICS BOOK #1

Enigmatic Biblical Phenomena with Possibility of Interpretation: Day One – Before The Flood

Message of Jesus #1

Proclamation of the Kingdom of Heaven on Earth as Primary Objective

NEW LIFE In 3 Priorities of T R I U M P H
Transformation ABC In The Kingdom of God